Unavailable:

One Lesbian's Struggle with the Bisexuality of Other Women

Unavailable:

One Lesbian's Struggle with the Bisexuality of Other Women

by Angela Kelly

jms books

UNAVAILABLE

JMS Books LLC
10286 Staples Mill Rd. #221
Glen Allen, VA 23060
www.jms-books.com

Printed in the United States of America

ISBN: 978-1-45658-700-0

"RESEARCHERS HAVE BEGUN to explore and identify various gradations in sexual orientation identity, paying attention to alternative sexual identity categories and attempting to clarify potential subtypes of same-sex sexuality, particularly among women. This study utilizes both quantitative and qualitative data to explore the behavioral experiences and identity development processes among women of a particular sexual identity subtype, 'mostly straight.'

"Participants were 349 female college students whose primary sexual identities included exclusively straight, mostly straight, bisexual, and lesbian. Results indicated that, on most behavioral variables, mostly straight women fell directly between and were significantly different from exclusively straight and bisexual/lesbian women.

"Mostly straight women were also distinct from exclusively straight women but were similar to bisexual women and lesbians on several quantitative measures of identity. Narratives about sexual identity development for mostly straight women revealed the complexities of sexual identity exploration, uncertainty, and commitment within this population.

"As a whole, this study encourages researchers to begin to recognize and examine 'mostly straight' as a distinct sexual identity subtype in young women."

From Thompson, E. M., & Morgan, E. M.
"'Mostly straight' young women:
Variations in sexual behavior and identity development."
Developmental Psychology, 44(1), 15-21.
Copyright © 2008 by the American Psychological Association.
Reproduced with permission.

For Liz, the only chapter I could not write.

Acknowledgments

I WOULD LIKE to thank all of my friends and family for their support in both my life and my writing. Of particular note, I want to thank JMS Books LLC, for making the publication of my first book a very easy and seamless process, JMS herself was with me every step of the way.

Some people in my life deserve special note and among them I extend sincere gratitude to Cindy Nichols, Cheri Peterson, Sara J. Rose, and Pam Crews. I would also like to say thanks for listening to my unending chatter about the subjects in this book to Dawn Nickens, Kate Maduzia, Kristen Hill, Julie Nichols, Sarah Kretchmer, Jane Cuvelier, Doris Bonnett, Cathy Garner, Jeanann Pumphrey, Jessy Johnson, Linda Zukowski, and all the angels at 718 South Randolph Street.

Angela Kelly

Contents

Introduction: The Unsures

IF YOU PICKED this book off the shelf because of its title, you probably need to read it as much as I needed to write it. My stories are by no means unique; my relationship experience is quite likely written on some of the same pages as your own.

If you are a lesbian, it is highly unlikely you haven't come across the women I refer to as "the unsures." Perhaps you had a different name for them or found these women in your own life to be indefinable by words alone. The unsures go beyond the bisexual realm. I exist in a world where, for myself, I could only ever imagine having been born gay or straight. By my own definition, being a lesbian does not mean I cannot appreciate male beauty, personality characteristics, or even sexual appeal. But it does mean I know beyond the shadow of a doubt I will not "wind up with" a male partner someday. Within my heart, I just *know*. Gay people of both sexes understand this. As it turns out, the rest of the world does not.

We live in an age of sexual revolution and a redefining of the concept of gender which is, in and of itself, a good thing. Most people actually don't live in the head space or even emotional space I do, where gay and straight exist in a clear-cut dichotomy. There is a lot of room between points A and B. The women in these stories fall at varying points on the in-between. From bisexual and bi-curious to sexually uncertain and—my personal favorite—"mostly" straight.

I wish you peace as you join me on the journey of these pages. If you have lived my experience, know you are okay as you are. At the end of the day, I still believe we can't really pick who we'll fall in love with. That is the very magic beneath these stories. Through it all, there is something very pure underneath. Something like love.

Chapter 1: Laying the Foundation
(The Ellen Trainer Experience)

I HAVE DEVELOPED a theory over the years that gay people are even more afraid of rejection than straight people because it is highly likely our very first experience of interest in another was with someone straight. What that means is most of us had our first experience of "love" with someone unavailable to us. It's a setup to be denied and feel rejected from the very beginning.

When I was in the 5th grade, I had my first recognizable crush on someone in the 8th grade. Later in life I understood I'd had crushes on teachers, my sister's friends, the checkout girl, etc. But this girl actually existed in my universe, which was school, and was someone I actually had conversations with and interacted with. I found myself thinking about nothing and no one else. There was a constant internal movie of where she was, what she said, how she looked, what she smelled like. At the tender age of eleven, I had not one clue what it all meant. All I knew was I sought her out, and I looked forward to running into her in the hallways with great anticipation. Her name was Ellen Trainer; her friends and sports team companions simply called her "The Train," or just plain "Train."

The Train seemed to enjoy the attention she got from me. I was called upon to run many an errand and perform multiple tasks for my beloved, all to my great joy. There was the borrowing of money or my Walkman and the carrying of books. Every now and then, for five minutes at a time, we'd be alone together, talking. It would take many more years for me to identify the feelings I had in those moments—I was falling in love. That is, whatever the eleven-year-old version of falling in love feels and looks like. Once in a very great while, she allowed me to touch her, hug her, or stand behind her and rub her shoulders. I knew nothing of sexual arousal, only that touching her was very intoxicating, even addictive.

I was a nerdy kid. Too smart for my peers, I sought friendships with my teachers. It just so happened that the 8th grade English teacher was a neighbor of mine, so I had occasion to befriend her long before I would be in her class. A writer from the time I was six—I have an old photograph of me at that age in front of a manual typewriter—I had already learned how to express myself and communicate through the written word. Spurred by my obsession with Trainer, I had what I believed at the time was a stroke of genius. I would write a short story about my love for The Train, and I would get Mrs. Johnson to read it to her class, thereby reading it to Ellen. Of course I would change her name, but she would know it was about her. Then, magically, she would come to me to fulfill my innocent crush fantasy once she understood how utterly devoted I was to her. It was perfect.

I wish I had that short story today, but I don't. I can't recall the details of what I wrote, only that the climax of the story was a long awaited hug full of meaning and emotion. Had I known I would have a future of writing for and about other women ahead of me, I might have tucked it away to remember where it all began. You know what they say about hindsight. In any case, I wrote my masterpiece.

The other part of this drama I will never understand is why Mrs. Johnson, a grown-up person, agreed with me that this fashion of proclaiming my love for Trainer was a good idea. In her defense, I'm quite sure I was a precocious child, and my eleven-year-old reasoning was bound to be passionate and irrefutable.

The day came when I knew Mrs. Johnson was going to read my story to her 8th grade class. How she worked that into her syllabus, I will never know. I couldn't concentrate in any of my own classes, awaiting what I was certain would be a miraculous turn of events. Visions of Mrs. Johnson's entire class moved to tears and brought to their feet with applause filled my head.

However, what really happened was The Train slowly sank further and further into her seat in that classroom, embarrassed in that way only teenagers can feel. The fact I had carefully changed names to hide both of our identities didn't matter— everyone in the room knew who the story was about. All of Trainer's friends had watched me follow her around like a puppy for months, standing by awaiting orders to fulfill her slightest demand. It never occurred to me I was being mocked, or even pitied. Her friends only ever saw one side; they were not there in our beautiful moments alone, and didn't see how she made me feel special, even chosen. They didn't understand.

Apparently, neither did Ellen Trainer.

In my adult life, the feelings of that time have all but washed away. Surely there are things about then I have blocked from my memory entirely. What I do remember is Ellen Trainer never spoke to me again, and from that moment on there was snickering in the girls' locker room when I went to gym class. The words "dyke" and "lezzie" worked their way into my vocabulary by the 6th grade. Well, not so much *my* vocabulary as the vocabulary of others directed at me.

Growing up gay is hard—it's amazing to me how many of us survive. When I was that young, and what made the Ellen Trainer experience so devastating was, as far as I knew of myself, I was straight. Having many other emotional defects at the time, the last thing I needed was another strike against my mental health. I had never had what most children have, that kind of life-long best friend that is so common in most people's lives. The classic American buddy, the one who accompanied you to the movies and the mall, slept over your house, took all the same classes in high school. I was deprived of such a playmate, save a few fragmented variations of such a companion. As a result, even when those kids began teasing me in the 6th grade, calling me by homophobic slurs more often than my own name, I truly believed all I wanted was a best friend like everyone else. Today I understand that masked the desire to not so much have what they had but to be like them, never comprehending what made me so different.

So I thought I wanted Ellen to be my best friend. My homosexuality was obviously apparent to a great number of people long before it was recognizable to me. I know that's not an uncommon phenomenon among us queers. Was Ellen an unsure? Maybe, maybe not. I doubt she knew any more about her own emotional and sexual inner workings at fourteen than I did at eleven. More likely she was just a bully teenager taking advantage of a younger child. However, although my own understanding of matters of sexuality did not come until I myself was sixteen, there was a pattern born from the Ellen Trainer experience. I met a girl who was not like me, became very attached and, at the cost of my own emotional well-being, pursued her in whatever way I knew how. Yet, as would be the case in many experiences to come, she was unavailable.

Chapter 2: Liza
"You really know how to seduce somebody."

MY HIGH SCHOOL years were primarily consumed by one girl-friend who actually was gay like me. Incidentally, she also had another girlfriend, so she was an unsure of a different variety, which I may write about in the future.

So my next unavailable came at my time of being not quite a girl but not yet a woman. I believe I was eighteen or nineteen. I have a sibling, a sister five years my senior. At that time, she was an undergraduate at a four year university. She belonged to a sorority, and one of her "social consciousness" activities was tutoring and mentoring young women disadvantaged or under-privileged due to social and economic status. Innocently enough, my sister came to me and said, "I was hoping you could help me, as she's closer to your age than mine. She just moved here with her mom and her baby and she doesn't know anyone. I thought you could take her out, introduce her to your friends, show her a good time."

I agreed, trying to be kind in what I believed to be an un-kind world. I really didn't think too much about it, until my sister brought her home to dinner.

It had been just another day until this jet black-haired vixen strode casually into my parent's living room. Lust was instantaneous, although this was another phenomenon I wouldn't understand for many years—in the early days I foolishly assumed everything was about love and "real" feelings. I shook her hand and introduced myself, saying my sister had told me a lot of wonderful things. Before long, my family sat down to dinner with this new center of my focus. I didn't say much—my parents were asking her a lot of questions, where was she from, what about her family, tell us about the baby, etc., etc. I could care less about the baby or her past. I just wanted to know when we were going out and imagined what it would be like to kiss her.

She spoke of an abusive ex-husband, which tripped my already well-formulated hero complex. Liza had walked a hard road—she was "disadvantaged," as my sister had said. Not the most eloquently spoken woman I'd ever met, but you could tell that, even for a lack of education, she was smart in that way many people with higher education could never be—life-smart, street-smart, which fascinated me. Keep in mind I come from a typical suburban upper middle class background.

Yes, Liza and I were definitely on opposite sides of the tracks. That made her even more attractive. I had a little "bad girl" fetish. If this story had taken place today, I probably would have described her as "Goth." After dinner, my sister asked if I'd drive Liza home. Of course I would.

We arrived at her apartment to find her mother and her newborn already asleep in the bedroom. She disappeared into the darkness for a few moments, and I could hear her whispering to her mother that a new friend her mentor introduced her to was in the living room, and we were going to stay up and talk for a while. She changed, then came back out in one of those satiny negligee things I would never in my life have the body to wear. I sat at a safe distance on the couch while she poured me a glass of cheap wine. Before long, she told me her whole relationship story, about the baby's father and a handful of other men before, during, and after her marriage. The more she talked, the more I felt that tug, that desire to nurture, to care for, to protect and "save." I didn't say anything for a long time, only occasionally reassuring her not all people were bad, and she would find those to help and be kind to her. She said, "Well, I guess that's true, since you just met me and you're already here."

She asked about my own relationship back story which, although short, had all the lesbian chaos and drama you'd expect. As I spoke, I watched for her reaction—I had no idea if she'd figured out I was gay, or if my sister had clued her in to what I find a relatively important detail about me. She did not seem phased, bothered, or the slightest bit uncomfortable. As a matter of fact, when I had vulnerably spilled my own emotional life (for I didn't yet know some people are not safe to be vulnerable with), she told me she'd thought about women, fantasized about women, and was every now and again attracted to women. I know now this is actually a relatively common conversation between allegedly heterosexual women and their lesbian friends, but at the time it struck me as a fucking miracle.

Somehow, as our conversation about feelings and lost love became more and more intimate, we became physically closer and closer on the couch, then graduated to the running of fingers through hair. Straight women do not understand how sexually and emotionally charged everyday affection can be for a lesbian woman. That's what makes these particular relationships so hard. Of course, I learned later on it's the lesbian's responsibility to set healthy boundaries. But I didn't know anything about boundaries then—I knew how to be impulsive, to act, and to not think about long-term consequences. So I kissed her.

To my utter delight, she kissed me back, and well, at that. "My mother would kill me," she said.

I replied, "Your mother doesn't have to know," and kissed her again.

Then she said, "You really know how to seduce somebody."

We made out for a while, and I didn't think I could get away with taking it any further than that so I didn't try. She asked me to stay with her. I did. We slept on blankets and comforters and couch cushions on the floor. I held her in my arms and gently stroked her face until she was asleep and I was in love.

I awoke to a blood-curdling infant scream. You might say I'm "not a kid person." I had a crick in my neck but a joy in my heart. I'd spent the past several years involved with a woman on and off who was no good for me, and was rarely good *to* me. When I wasn't with her, I'd been mixed up with a woman twice my age, who was also not particularly good for me, other than she made me feel desired and cherished in a way the other woman did not. Yet here was Liza, a woman untainted by prior relationships with other women. This I could do.

Of course, I was under the assumption that now, after making out and sleeping side by side, we were actually having a romantic relationship. I knew no other reality apart from that. Having met my first female lover when I was fifteen, I knew nothing about dating or getting to know each other, building a partnership and growing together. I had dated boys, but even when I was trying to do that, I followed the same formula—it just took much less time for it to unravel.

So there I was, the morning after what I thought was simply a swell beginning. All the getting to know each other required had already occurred as far as I was concerned. I noticed she wasn't really paying much attention to me, barely making eye contact. I stayed anyway, desperate to be near her, and had breakfast with Liza, her mom, and her baby, just like a family. Although she seemed distant and uncomfortable, I wrote that off as, "Well, of course, she doesn't want her mother to know she's a lesbian." Because she kissed me with enthusiasm, and more than once, I foolishly assumed she *was* a lesbian.

I am a self-centered person—most of us are, particularly when we're younger. It never occurred to me this woman had been abused, manipulated, and used by others, particularly men, her whole life. I hadn't one clue about what it meant to have a child, to have no choice in caring for a little, defenseless person who depended on you to have all of its needs met. The concept of having missed out on one's own young adulthood eluded me completely.

When I looked at this woman, I only saw one thing—a person I must be with because I couldn't imagine not being with her after kissing her. It never dawned on me our little make-out session could have been just a one time event. Never once did I think this person was by no means relationship material, let alone myself. She was just damaged enough for me to want to fix her, to take care of her; fucking her was actually secondary to all of that.

This sheer codependency of mine would prove to stay with me for the better part of my life. Somehow I knew if I could get a woman to "need" me, the chances of her leaving me decreased dramatically.

So I set out on a rigorous course of making myself indispensable. I brought dinner, helped with child, helped her study, did the dishes, cleaned her apartment, drove her wherever she needed to go, which included Brooklyn on a few occasions. When I am in love—or, at least, my understanding of that phrase—all things beside the object of my affection take a back burner immediately.

I can still be responsible, mind you; I was a student at the time and continued to go to class and study. And friendship has always been undeniably important, so I kept the few close friends I had. Beyond that, though, my whole life was dedicated to trying to get this woman to a) have sex with me, and b) love me. I believed one was a natural consequence of the other.

The next few times we saw each other after that morning with her mother, she rebuffed my innuendos, turned away when I tried to kiss her, and wouldn't so much as hug me but for a brief second or two. That was all fine—she was new to the lesbian thing and I knew it would take time. So I backed off, let her have her space (however much space one can have when I'm at her house every day), and played the role of "friend." I had my hands full juggling my ex-but-sometimes-not and my free-pot-giving butch dyke who was old enough to be my mother.

In between, I courted Liza, who was far more beautiful to me than the other two and therefore deserved more of my attention. This was my ethical scale. There is something very ego-based about being with a woman not only I, but most other people, consider attractive. The desire to be vindicated by those "hotter" than myself is really a matter of self-worth. Looks become irrelevant at some point, and years later I realized all I have done over and over and over is settle for less, because I believed I wasn't worth more.

The time frame is hazy in my memory, but a few things co-incided. First, I'd essentially given up on ever working things out with my ex since she started sleeping with my pot-giving butch dyke surrogate mother. This allowed me the time to do what my sister had originally intended, which was build up Liza's social network. Within about a month, my friends became her friends and I quite cunningly wove her into the fabric of my everyday life. Since she was the one with the baby, our partying took place mostly at her apartment. Aside from one or two real lifetimers, my "friends" were people who would drink copious amounts of alcohol and get stoned with me. She was a fairly responsible mother—I never remember seeing her really drunk but, then again, I was drunk most of the time, so I'm not sure I would have noticed.

In any event, my friends adored her as much as I did, particularly Jack, who I had actually tried to make my boyfriend, but, for obvious reasons, that wasn't working out. When I realized they were into each other, I sort of "gave" him to her. Anything to make her happy, so said my martyrdom. By then she was dangling just enough carrots to keep me hooked—she'd reverted to the occasional kiss on the corner of the mouth, and would sleep with me about once a week, curled up like a cat in my arms. This surely meant she was recognizing my value as a partner, and would come around soon enough. Jack was a good guy, but only I really knew what she needed, and that did not come attached to a penis.

I became Liza's whipping post, and by then it was too late for me to be able to swiftly overcome my feelings for her. She both needed and resented my attraction to her, so she would lead me on one minute and the next tell me I was fat and she found me repulsive. I didn't know this was a form of abuse. I don't know if she knew this was a form of abuse. But abuse it was, and I suffered it like any self-imposed victim would do. Jack eventually grew tired of her manipulation, and even tried to explain how she was taking advantage of me. I thought, "No, she just doesn't love you Jack, but me, she does love me."

What basis of fact I had for this, I've no idea—those tender moments one hangs onto, I suppose, such as the vulnerable tears when she admitted to needing me on many occasions over the course of that year. I gave her a lot of slack; in my memory of her I still do. What background did she come from? What did she know about making her way in the world as a responsible adult, or having relationships with other adults? Surely no more than I did at the time—we were children with adult liquor habits and unknown codependency issues at best.

So I stayed. I couldn't deny that I wasn't as "in love" with her as I once was—my feelings vacillated between lust and resentment on a fairly continual basis. I'd come face to face with my own issues of sexuality, and was compulsively both dating and sleeping with men, only to return to her, needful and seeking to fill an emptiness no man could have fulfilled. It was the perfect addicted lesbian tragedy.

Liza was in contact with her ex-husband more and more— he was seemingly trying to buy her back with gifts and cards and random child support when he had it. With me she had developed a new fetish of dressing me up like a doll, doing my hair and makeup—I suppose somehow trying to justify her attraction to me, for if I were "pretty," it was okay she wanted to have sex with me. In my ripped jeans, bandannas, and T-shirts, my image was unacceptable to her. I allowed this because I believed it would grant me access to her bed which, at this point, was all I was really interested in. To hell with loving her—that got me nowhere. But fucking her, now that would be satisfying after all the energy I'd put into this dysfunctional partnership.

One night she called and asked me to come over. To my surprise, I was greeted at the door by Alex, her ex-husband, who shook my hand and gave me a beer. Alex was not at all what I envisioned him to be. Yes, he had a classic biker look about him in his leather apparel, as Liza had described him, but he was short, skinny, and not particularly attractive. Because I found her to be incredibly hot, I assumed she would only have ever been involved with equally hot men. Apparently that wasn't the case, and my very first thought was, "And *I'm* not pretty enough for her?" In any event, I rolled with the evening which, to the observer, would have looked just like three friends partying together. To a keener observer, it probably looked like the episode of a Jerry Springer show. I didn't know where the baby was, and I didn't ask.

You know where this is going, don't you? I did, too. I wish I could give you a hot and steamy sex scene, but a) it really wasn't, and b) I don't remember much of it after so many years and sexual escapades later. What I do recall is we were all fairly intoxicated and somehow wound up all sort of entangled on the couch together. When Alex left the room to use the bathroom (or maybe put on a condom?), I looked at Liza and said, "I don't think I can do this."

She kissed me and whispered in my ear, "This is the only way you will ever have me." Then she took me by the hand and led me into the bedroom.

When Alex joined us on the bed, I was coherent enough to set some ground rules, just in case he had any disillusions about sexual contact between him and me. He was fine with that and simply said, "This is all about her."

Agreed. He quietly stroked himself while he watched his ex-wife and mother of his child make out with me for what seemed like a long time. I undressed her slowly, exploring her body in exactly the way I'd imagined doing so many times. She, in turn, undressed me, and Alex undressed himself while I wasn't paying attention.

To his credit, he did have a nice sized dick—I could see why she enjoyed sex with him. He went down on her for a time while we continued to stroke each other's bodies and kiss. I kept waiting for her to touch me between my legs, but she didn't. She kissed me and kissed me, ran her nails down my back, sucked my nipples, but she refused to do the ultimate lesbian act, which pissed me off, and I became preoccupied with being pissed off.

When Alex became bored with oral sex, he mounted her. She would still kiss me and touch me, but by then I really just wanted to have an orgasm. So I led her hand to the place where I thought she should be and she acquiesced. The problem, though, was twofold: 1) she had really long fingernails, not at all conducive to lesbian digital sex, and 2) she was inexperienced, and really had no idea what she was doing. I was losing her focus while her ex-husband pumped away anyhow, so ultimately I rolled away from both of them and masturbated while I watched them have sex. Relieved to have an orgasm, I simply got up and left the room.

This was not how it was supposed to be. This was not at all what I had signed up for in catering to this woman for over a year. I sat naked in the living room wondering where I had gone wrong in my seduction of her. Angry, I drank whatever alcohol was left in the house while I listened to the person I wanted to be my lover scream in ecstasy with a man who had beaten and abandoned her on more than one occasion. This, I decided in a rare moment of clarity, was insanity. I left my would-be lover and her husband to their own dysfunction and drove home.

For a couple of weeks, maybe months, I still had contact with her. Somewhere along the line she became an occasional pot dealer to me, and our relationship drifted to one of business rather than emotion. She tried every now and again to captivate me as she once had, trying to find her way back into my heart and lure me sexually, but I had crossed a threshold in a direction away from her that could not be traveled again.

I eventually returned to my butch, who I would never be seen with in public but in private reassured me I was more desirable than my ex, whom she had stopped seeing. Over the course of the next couple of years, I did find firm footing about my own homosexuality, and I cut men loose altogether. When I began writing this book, I hadn't thought about Liza in a very long time—it's as if I'm writing about someone else's life. Still, there were moments where the old pain rose to the surface, and I could see clearly the thread of some of my more glaring character flaws that ran through this unsure relationship and all the ones to follow. I had a lot to learn ahead of me, even though I left Liza behind.

Chapter 3: Tina
"How well can you lie?"

IT'S HAPPENED TO the best of us. Living our lives as gay, we have sworn never to get involved with a straight woman. However, one day, it happens. Completely unannounced, out of the blue. When we first realize our attraction to the forbidden, we think, "Okay, so, I want her. I'll get over it."

Then, against our will, we fall head over heels. We know they aren't like us—they tell us constantly. They continually profess their straightness, even when they begin waking up in our beds. Still, we cling to our thin fragments of hope—that love conquers all, that they are just afraid and will overcome it, that this is the woman we will someday propose to. It doesn't usually happen that way. Even if she turns out to actually be gay, it's always with some other woman instead of us. Why do we take these risks? How do we let these love tragedies happen? I'll tell you how.

There once was a girl who worked in my store. It doesn't really matter how we crossed paths or where she came from. All I know is it started as something completely innocent; as these things often do. One day I was upset about something, probably boss-related, and she was the unfortunate one to find me crying at my desk. Upon discovering me, she came to my rescue and dried my tears, as any decent woman would. We became fast friends after that event, and within weeks discovered a common thread. As it turned out, she was a friend of a co-worker named Julia. It just so happened a co-worker friend of mine, Rick, really had a thing for Julia. So we set out to play matchmakers and arranged for the four of us to go out for drinks.

Again, this was a completely innocent rendezvous. However, it did present the opportunity to tell my life story, as I am so fond of doing. Contrary to the usual, my story didn't frighten her, shock her, or make her cry. These are the most common responses, although once I actually sent a woman screaming from the room. That first night out, I felt a slow, creeping sensation the closer I got to her, and I quickly decided to ignore it and plead insanity to my internal moral judges. I completely lost interest in the outcome of Julia and Rick, which was supposedly why we were out in the first place. Was that really why? Of course not, I knew myself all too well. However, I succeeded in playing it off, and was content Tina was quite clueless about my inner struggle.

We continued to hang out after work frequently, sometimes with other co-workers, sometimes Julia and Rick, sometimes Rick and some other member of his harem. Obviously, Julia and Rick never did get together for this reason. Eventually, though, as fate would have it, the ritual became just her and me.

How convenient.

I had realized weeks earlier how I really felt about Tina, and chose to ignore it. When I could no longer ignore it, I opted not to speak about it…at least, not to her. I had never fallen for someone so straight. Of course, I had fallen for women that were "confused," but that was different. This woman was grounded; she really knew who she was. Out of the people I knew, she was by far the most together. Maybe that's why I fell. I needed someone like her to keep me in line. I realized at this point in my life I was Freudian after all; I looked for a mother figure.

I kept my promise to myself about not saying anything to Tina of how I felt, but I knew I was showing it whenever we were together, which rapidly became all the time. I felt consumed by her presence, enveloped in her proximity. She was truly a beautiful woman. She had the kind of face that, in the right light, represented an angel's features, almost too perfect to touch. I couldn't help but stare into her eyes, which always seemed to be so guarded, so aware, and sometimes afraid. I now knew what it was like to be so in love with someone, that when you look upon them, you are suddenly unable to speak.

All the while, in the midst of my passion, I could not shake the feeling there was something there, in her, for me. I couldn't understand. When we were together, I asked about her boyfriend a lot, and all of her volunteered information seemed to suggest she was very happy where she was. I couldn't help but wonder why she was with me so much of the time if things were so good. Between two jobs and me, I don't know when she found time for him. Not that I was complaining, mind you.

One night while we were out sobering up in a diner, the inevitable inquisition came. I think subconsciously we went out and drank as often as we did so if anything ever *did* happen between us, we could blame it on alcohol. While trying desperately to think about something other than kissing her, she blatantly asked, "So, how do you feel about me?"

I wanted to crawl under the table and die. I'm not a very good liar, and there was absolutely no way around such a direct question. I tried the best I could to get out of it anyway. I composed myself, sat up straight, avoided her gaze, and said, "I don't think there's anything that needs to be said."

As you may have guessed, she didn't let it go at that. Why did I have to fall in love with someone so direct? I played with the salt shaker and weighed my options. I could fake a heart attack, but I didn't think she'd buy it. Then again, I did take acting classes in college. As I was trying to figure out various escapes, she reached across the table and touched my hand.

Adrenaline rushed through every part of my body, then went straight to my brain. I thought for a moment I was having hot flashes. I lifted my head and she was looking directly at me. No, she was looking *through* me. I had to spill my guts or I'd never be able to live with myself. I felt so guilty and I hadn't even done anything.

When I was through speaking, her only response was, "But you know that it just…can't…be."

Of course I knew that. So then why were we having this conversation at all? Thoroughly humiliated at having been forced into confessions of my mortal sins, I decided I really needed to leave. I drove her back to her car in silence. There were no words to say.

When we finally did speak, we went on as if we had never discussed anything more than work and football. I told her I would come up and see her tomorrow and bring her some lunch. I was off but I had a ton of paperwork I could catch up on. Thus, the night it began was all over.

I drove home swearing we would never discuss how I felt about her ever again. A few days later, we were back at the bar. Then, sure enough, we were back at the diner, which some time later became affectionately known as "ours." This time, our discussion centered on the fact that, as much as she cared for me, she wasn't attracted to me.

Again, I wanted to crawl under the table and spend a few hours there. Resisting the urge, I quietly told myself she was just in denial. Then I realized it was me who was in denial. Over the years I had developed a talent for lying to myself under extreme circumstances—I'm quite good at it. I became very upset and had to excuse myself.

While I was in the bathroom, she had no idea I was crying in there; I hadn't let on that much. But I was frustrated. If she didn't feel a spark every time she touched me, then why did she touch me all the time? Or let me touch her? Why was touching allowed at all? It was that annoying borderline dividing a hug from more than a hug. I really hated those kinds of gray areas, and after my Liza experience years prior, I went to great lengths to avoid them.

When I went back to the table, she was sitting there with a forlorn look that said, "I didn't mean to hurt your feelings." I hate that. I just wanted to run away from her. She had the power to really hurt me, and I didn't want to be hurt anymore. My last girlfriend did enough damage to compensate for the entire female race.

But when we got outside, Tina looked so sad, so innocent and lost. How could I run away from that? I suddenly felt the rush of an emotional breakdown coming on and I tried to fight it with all my willpower. It was no use; the feeling was too strong. Before I could take it back, all my emotions, in one powerful statement, were out there just hanging in the wind. "I love you."

It had happened; I had become irrational. That's what I do when I'm in love, I can't help it. My heart becomes a two-ton ox while my intellect lies defeated like a crushed ant. I still don't know what it was Tina felt at that exact moment—only she could tell you which path she decided to take down "a lesbian loves me" road. Whatever forces moved her, that night they moved her to my side. She comforted me, consoled me, held me in her arms. All the things a lover would do, but also the things a good friend would do. There was that damned gray area again. The evening ended on an awkward note—I can't even recall the last words spoken. Though, at least this time, there were words to say.

Weeks later, we were in a constant state of being uncomfortable around each other. A new discussion was necessary. I knew having a heart to heart would be difficult because she wasn't like me, not as open, not as good with words. When our next big talk took place, the words she did decide to use were,

"How well can you lie?"

That alone should have been my cue to cut my losses and get out while I still could. But, being the individual I am, I took off after Tina in relentless pursuit. She had given me the green light the only way she knew how. And the green light was fine, as long as it was hidden from virtually everyone we knew.

The store where we worked wasn't far from her hometown, so all of our co-workers knew both her and her boyfriend; they had all gone to high school together. My work life from that day forth became somewhat of a nightmare. I was viewed in a negative light by everyone—all they saw was this poor, delusional lesbian in love with Tina, whom they all assumed I would never get. Little did they know, but I had to keep that lying promise I made in the company break room.

I tried not to think about what may or may not happen. I tried to forget she had a boyfriend of four years. I tried to have that "take what you can get" attitude. None of it was true. I knew I loved her, and I tried desperately to believe she loved me in return but was just scared. I no longer knew what was real and what was pure fantasy. Days after the "how well can you lie" comment, I kissed her for the first time.

That one action turned my whole world upside down. It felt so strange, like the first time I'd ever kissed another woman, which was so many years ago. I assume what she felt inside was the same, but she couldn't identify it the way I could. She had no prior experience to compare it to. I had no idea what was going to happen next.

What finally *did* happen was she took me to Atlantic City for the weekend. I had no idea how she got that past her boyfriend, but I didn't care to inquire. I was so content to have her all to myself for the first time, away from our everyday lives and everyone we knew. That weekend consummated the inevitable. I had no idea if she would concede to sharing a bed with me or not. It was a gamble; it could have gone either way.

When we turned out the lights, I felt like a nervous high

school virgin about to bang the star quarterback. After all, it had been quite some time for me, and I have always been self-conscious about my performance in bed (not that I had any complaints, mind you). I suppose the thrill of something totally new would have been enough to carry Tina through and satisfy her. As for me, sex really is like riding a bike—it always comes back to you even after years of not riding anything at all.

What took place in that hotel room is what I assume happens between lesbians and non-lesbians all over the world. There was enough high-wire thrill and pent-up passion where ecstasy was possible even without Tina's reciprocation. If you have ever been in this position, you know exactly what I mean. If you haven't, don't worry; it's not relative. All I wanted was for Tina to feel something she had never felt before. To this day, I'm still not sure if she did.

I started kissing her, and eventually began to undress her. She asked, "What are you doing?"

I'd have thought that was obvious. I didn't say anything and kissed her nipples instead, having that distinct moment when you feel your partner's pulse quicken, hear their breathing change, and know what you wanted to happen so desperately is finally going to play itself out. We were both a little drunk and the pressure was so enormous, sex between us was awkward at best. Not bad, just a little strange. I used my best tricks with my hands inside her body, and it didn't take long for her to reach orgasm. I came from the sheer exhilaration of having given her pleasure. That turned out to be a very good thing because, much to my disappointment, Tina did not reciprocate the act of lovemaking.

This was to become a theme. Tina and I continued to have sex, but all that really meant was I continued to make love to her and she never touched me—at least, not where it counts. She would kiss me, that was it. Without having to speak about it, she inherently understood having a leg to rub up against was just fine for me. I was so excited by her, so attracted to her, I didn't need her to touch my genitals to get off.

Still, it would have been nice. Once, and only once, I followed the advice of a callous friend who told me, "Just grab her hand." That was bad advice. When I did that, and tried to forcefully get her to concede to my sexual wishes, she totally freaked out. I felt like a rapist and, that day, neither of us came. I spent several weeks groveling in apology.

I fell deeper and deeper and things got harder and harder as a result. I continued to believe she loved me, even though she couldn't tell me. I was aware of how unhealthy our relationship was, and how obsessive I had become. I guess deep in my heart I knew it would never work. But I couldn't bring myself to leave her, mostly out of my own insecurity and fear I would not be missed. She equally could not leave me, partly because I wouldn't let her, and partly because through it all she really did care, and knew how much she would hurt me.

I had moments of hope, particularly after she finally did break up with her boyfriend. All along I had been fulfilling emotional needs of hers he had not been meeting, and I knew this was my vantage point. I thought perhaps our sex life would fall into place after she got used to the idea, and until then my best offense was to win her over romantically. I wrote her poetry, seduced her with mixed tapes (still a romantic staple in that day), professed my undying love for eternity, showered her with gifts, exhausted all financial and emotional resources…pleasing and catering to her became my life's work.

At that time, my version of "winning someone over" was really nothing more than emotional blackmail beneath all my perceived "giving." Every time I thought she was going to call things off, I played the depression/suicidal card. I trapped her into relationship with me and took her hostage. Our whole romance revolved around alcohol and crying more often than not.

Having my dysfunctional heartbreak history already well established into my early twenties, I still had no clue what relationship or even love actually meant. I did love Tina, but I loved her only in a way that reflected my understanding of the day. Who teaches a young lesbian about love? You would think other lesbians, of course. Yet my partnership life to date included only other psychotic maladjusted lesbians who also knew nothing of intimacy, trust, or mutual respect. I took what I had learned into my relationship with Tina, and was woefully low on positive reference points.

There were many attempts, mostly hers, to bring things to a close. My attempts were always for spite, head games to prove a point. I know I can be quite manipulative when I put my mind to it. When reality set in, however, I knew there were differences we could never reconcile. The most important issue was that Tina was, after all, not gay, and I knew that all along deep down inside. If she had been, we might have made it.

Unfortunately, life is never that easy. Real love is eventually what did allow me to set her free. I cared about Tina, and knew she had so much guilt, she could never stay with me out of anything other than retribution. Somewhere I had discovered enough self-respect to want to be with someone who also wanted to be with me. I no longer wanted a partner I had won over with trickery and manipulation.

I have forgiven her because she did always tell me the truth. I knew she was straight, I knew she had a boyfriend. I knew that "it could never be," she told me herself. But it was, it did happen. Despite all of the denial, mine and hers, it happened. I loved her, and I believe in her own way, she loved me. I suppose it was just something that started out simple, then turned into more than either of us bargained for.

The point is, this kind of love is not something I recommend. It's true there are women who do what Tina did and wake up and say, "Hey, this is great. This is what I've been looking for—this is me." However, let the truth be known, there are just as many women who say, "Hey, I could be happy and comfortable here, but this isn't how I want to live my life."

One of the best responses to a gay issue question I ever

heard was by a female writer whose name I unfortunately cannot recall. She was asked why she was gay and her response was, "If the first person I truly fell in love with was a man, I would be straight, but it wasn't." Tina spent almost a year in a relationship with me being unsure. I myself didn't know what love was until I loved a woman. Tina knew what love was because she had, at one time, loved her boyfriend. Because of conflicting interests, we could never love each other.

Chapter 4: Jennifer
"It's the way you look at me."

NO HISTORY OF unsuccessful bisexual romances would be complete without falling in love with a stripper. Okay, maybe it would be for some people, but not for me.

In March of 2003, my existence was a living hell. I'd left my wife of seven years right after the holidays but, due to financial circumstances, we were still co-habitating. My ex-wife was dating by then and, ironically, her new girlfriend and I hit it off. Both during and after our marriage, my ex and I remained sort of friends, mostly because we were bonded by our mutual love of drugs and alcohol. Myself, the ex, and the ex's new partner (all truly gay, by the way) also had many mutual friends, as is often the case in any small lesbian community, so the three of us spent time together socially.

Then the ex and the new girlfriend became serious, withdrawing into that world only honeymoon couples can know. I wasn't jealous about my ex; after all, it was I who left her. But new-love bliss is unbearable to witness for any forlorn single person. Loneliness arrived, along with the harsh reality of a failed marriage immediately followed by an impassioned, lustful affair with a bisexual woman that was doomed from the start. I fell rapidly into the abyss known primarily by its medical name—depression. Those of you who can empathize understand saying, "I'm depressed," is often the understatement of a lifetime.

Saint Patrick's Day was the most horrific I'd endured since my trials began. I sobbed uncontrollably without warning. I couldn't work, eat, sleep, or perform any other day-to-day activity that should come as naturally as drawing breath. Soon I found myself with little desire to do even that. I left work at lunchtime with no plans to return, then did all the things that would normally make me feel better—took a drive, wrote some pages, shot some film.

Nothing helped. Giving up, I went home to drink. The happy couple took pity on me. Leaving for dinner, they promised to call so I could meet them somewhere for green beer. That was at 6:00 P.M. By 9:30 they hadn't called and I was drunk and determined to have the company of a woman. I planned to head to campus in search of intoxicated, unsuspecting, bi-curious college girls.

Driving to the ATM for can-I-buy-you-a-drink-cash, I abandoned the college girl plan, remembering it was a twenty-year old who had ripped my heart from my chest without remorse. I contemplated the local landscape, then recalled I'd pretty much seen all there was to see of my town's lesbian scene without being impressed. Suddenly I had a blinding revelation. A voice in my head shouted, "*Go to the strip club!*" Sure, I'd be paying for the privilege of affection, but at least I knew what to expect and wouldn't go home disappointed.

I walked defiantly into the club, as any lesbian alone would, with renewed enthusiasm. I'd been before, but only with my ex back when we had friends who worked there. I sat down feeling the eyes of heterosexual men upon me, but I used to frequent a similar club back in Jersey so I was used to it. Regardless of

Saint Patrick, business was slow, I gathered there were maybe six or eight girls present in all. The bartender was friendly, giving me a knowing smile, increasing my sense of comfort. I kept my back to the stage and the half-nakedness upon it, amused by my own behavior. Glancing around, I awaited the reaction. In my experience, if a lesbian's in a strip club, one of two things will occur—either a stripper is markedly enthusiastic about women, or she'll avoid them like the plague.

After nursing my second beer and chain-smoking half a pack of cigarettes, my zeal fizzled. Physical and emotional energy were depleted and I sensed the plague scenario. The woman I found most visually appealing didn't even glance in my direction, and the ones who did didn't interest me. Just as I was grabbing my car keys, there was a hand on my knee. Never will I forget those first words: not "hi," "hello," or "how are you this evening?" Instead, she asked earnestly, "Are you okay?"

I turned to see a woman I *had* noticed earlier, initially because she reminded me of the girl who left me. She didn't necessarily look like her but had similar features, hair, and body type. When she spoke, I detected an air of genuine kindness and concern. Smiling, I answered, "Do I not look okay?"

She said, "Well, you seem deep in thought." Her name was Sunrise. After extended strip club experience, I still forgot the pointlessness of inquiring when any customer will only ever be granted a pseudonym.

Nevertheless, Sunrise carried a tangible presence with her I was drawn to at once. I plunged into my tragic story in spite of knowing this opening conversation was part of a typical routine. She sat next to me for over an hour, leaving me only once for her performance, which I watched with dreamlike enchantment.

Afterward she returned, never once appearing uninterested or concerned about other patrons. Slowly I became aware of a tremendous feeling of release. It wasn't I had no one to talk to; I still had a few friends who were unconditionally supportive. Yet I always felt I had to explain myself or justify my actions. To use a common cliché, I felt like no one understood, until then.

The night slipped silently by and the inevitable question came. "So, do you want a dance?"

Shyly I said, "I haven't been in here in a long time. How much?"

Matter-of-factly she replied, "Ten bucks."

I pushed the eighteen dollars on the bar toward her, saying, "This is all the money I have." In response to her skeptical look, I assured her, "I don't mean in the world, just what I have with me."

Taking my hand, she led me to the mirror-lined fantasy land behind the DJ booth. The moment she touched me, I realized I'd been starving for mere human contact. I felt a sensation that should be reserved only for someone I was actually involved with, not a stranger and certainly not a stripper. Still, I couldn't deny its familiarity.

I drove home that night a changed person, shaken by the sheer force of passion I had believed was lost to me forever. This woman was very good at her job—for me, as a customer, it was because she understood the difference between sexuality and sensuality, and between physical desire and connected intimacy. What most strippers I'd had the pleasure of knowing over the years offered was much less than that. All perfectly beautiful and wonderful people, but the minimal effect of what they elicited I could achieve at home with a margarita and an adult web site for a lot less cash.

For the next 24 hours, I thought about little else besides the magical woman I'd met and, like the sleazy stalker all strippers come to despise, I went back night after night after night. Somehow I believed this was not typical, that my interaction with this woman was slightly more than customer/client from the very beginning. Along with the shoddy remains of a long-term relationship still festering, I was in an alcoholic or drug-induced fog much of the time, so I can't say my perceptions were entirely accurate.

Not having the resources to be a big spender in the club frequently, I'd hoard cash for about a week then blow it all in one night. I would only get dances from her, and if she wasn't there, I didn't stay. I wrote her letters and delivered them. I brought her marijuana and a burned mixed CD. She was the only thing in my life that brought any sort of happiness and my unrealistic fantasy had taken root deep within me. Like most people who fall under the spell of addiction, I chased her the same way I chased my drugs and alcohol. As a matter of fact, there came a point where on most paydays if I had to choose between illegal narcotics and her, she won. At the time I believed I had my drug addiction well hidden from view of most people, but my demand and dependence upon this Sunrise was obvious to anyone. I would find out later my other addictions were equally obvious, and this was actually to become a big part of my story with the stripper.

So dependent upon her to fulfill my emotional needs, I planned my 31st birthday party around her and the club and a couple of other dancers I'd become platonically friendly with. I invited all my so-called friends, including my ex-wife and her new lover. I figured the more people I could get to contribute to what I termed my "lap dance fund," the more time I would have with Sunrise and, by then, that was all I wanted, all I craved, the only single thing I looked forward to on any given day.

To date, aside from getting to be with her, it was the single worst birthday I have ever had. I had reached a point of really coming apart at the seams with my multitude of addictions and faced moving out of my broken home into a new place, a new future, single and scared to death. By the time the night I'd looked forward to with such anticipation finally arrived, I was a broken woman and it showed. Having already been up for two or three days, no amount of continued substance abuse was going to make me feel any better.

But I hoped against hope that she, this angel in my life, would. Inevitably, while getting my extended lap dance marathon at the end of the evening, I could not hold it together any longer. Over Sunrise's shoulder, I saw my ex-wife, sloppy drunk, belligerent, embarrassing. I saw the reality of my circumstances: a birthday with people I called friends who barely knew me; my dealer among them, whose gift to me was a shot of Crown Royal and a card with a free baggie of drugs taped to the inside; co-workers from a job I was very close to losing; the epitome of my failed marriage stumbling away toward the bar...all surrounded by the empty glasses and bottles I had drained in a desperate attempt to escape what I had become.

Pathetically, on top of it all, I could see my own reflection in the mirror-lined walls of the dancing area behind the DJ booth—a woman who, at that moment, had nothing and no one, who felt the closest to the person I was paying money to touch me whose real name I didn't even know. There was nothing left for me to do but what I did next. I wept.

Now I'm not sure how many dancers have had people cry while getting a lap dance, but I'd guess the percentage is low. I'm sure there are emotional men out there who may have done what I did, but I never met them. So I'm not sure what the typical dancer reaction to that might be. Sunrise, though, proved to be the angle of mercy I had believed. She didn't say a word for a long time, and instead just held me, ran her fingers through my hair, and let me cry. It no longer mattered to me if it was all an act for the sake of my $50 or $100 bills. Stripper or not, she gave me exactly what I needed in that moment, and she made me feel cared about, like I was worthy of being cared about, a belief I had lost somewhere in the life I was living.

This was my proof positive I needed to look no further for a partner. I wanted her and no one else. I saw a relationship with her as my way out of the one I was having with myself, which wasn't going very well, what with all the self-loathing and hatred. From that night on, I treated her as if she were really my girlfriend, minus things like dates, phone calls, actual time together. None of that mattered since the partnership existed mostly in my own head anyway.

For a little while, things were actually quite good, and it really did feel…real? Perhaps that's not the right word. We certainly had a connection of sorts—some people just have chemistry, she openly acknowledged that. The more convinced I became, the worse I behaved. We passed a turning point that probably largely rested on her seeing what was really happening to me, which in reality had nothing to do with her. I had "issues" long before I met Sunrise.

But if I had believed she was the solution, when she started setting boundaries, she became the problem. I interpreted waiting in line behind other customers a personal affront. Resentment grew as I felt her behavior with me become more and more stripper-like and less personal. I'd been vulnerable and now what? She wasn't going to be vulnerable with me? How dare she. I tried and tried and tried, pushed and pushed and pushed, and even started telling her I loved her. Looking back, I can't believe she never had me banned from the bar.

She put up with me for another month, maybe more. Then she sat me down and had "the talk." If you have ever been obsessed with a stripper, you are familiar with this talk. It is much more humiliating than any breakup could ever hope to be. Essentially, you are sat in a chair and told the proper business boundaries of what you're doing—that you are a client, and you are simply paying for a service. Any delusions you might have are essentially of your own making, and the object of your affection is simply doing a job, performing a task for a paycheck on a daily and weekly basis, just like you.

Admirably, she owned up to her own mistakes in our humble beginning, saying, "I don't know, maybe it's because you're a woman. But I have let you do things I would not even dream of letting other customers do." Meaning, presumably, writing her letters and burning her CDs and making time for me even when there was a line of higher paying customers ahead of me.

I became belligerent and drunk, since I didn't want her to

see I was embarrassed and ashamed. I was going to make my big move and give her my phone number that night, based on my insane belief she wanted it, so I tried to do so but not in a kind fashion. Instead, I waited for her to reject me, then said, "I think you won't take my number because you're actually afraid you might use it." And I left.

I was so angry I didn't return to the club for several weeks, and when I did, I ignored her and got dances from other girls. Making myself look like even more of a jerk than I did already was an expensive venture. My warped thinking was totally convinced I was right, that she was, if nothing else, attracted to me and it scared her, and that was *her* problem, not mine. I built my case, collecting all the evidence I had—conversations that far surpassed those of stripper/client, certain looks of affection which simply could not be feigned, personal details I was certain she wasn't sharing with any other customer, knowing more often than not I got at least a couple more dances than I had paid for.

I ignored the basics: she had a boyfriend, a fact I had verified by other strippers I had befriended; all of our interaction took place at the club and never anywhere else; and I was a drunken junkie trying desperately to find someone or something to save me from my personal hell.

The only good thing that came out of my attempt to stay away from her was I took a different stripper home from a party one night and she inadvertently told me Sunrise's real name. Jennifer. Of course, she assumed I knew. I also learned that, although we weren't and never would be, some other dancers and regular customers I'd befriended actually did assume we were having a relationship outside the club or, at least a remarkably intimate one inside of it.

That dancer I brought home with me actually said, "I know you're Jennie's girl and I don't want to step on anyone's toes." There is no rationale to it, but hearing that and knowing her real name made me feel closer to her. Coupled with the fact that no matter how much money I spent on drugs, alcohol, or other dancers, I truly missed her.

And it was not the lap dances I missed; it had gone far beyond that. What I was missing was actually *her*, not her body or how she touched me, although I enjoyed those things on a physical level. It was the way she laughed, the way she said my name, the feeling I got when I knew she'd turned someone else down because I was waiting patiently for her. Whether she would have admitted to it or not, there were nights when I walked in at closing time and she actually looked relieved to see me. So I went back to her.

I went to the club one night actually sober and worked up the courage to ask for a dance. Hanging out at the end of the bar waiting for her to walk by, I felt very foolish and remorseful. I knew enough about her by then to understand she had problems of her own—who was I to add drama at the strip club to the list? When I handed her cash, she looked at me and said, "So we're okay?"

Quite sure it wasn't exactly in the same way, I dared to believe maybe, just maybe, she'd missed me too.

It was as if there had been no interruption. We picked up whatever real relationship (what else can I call it?) we were building exactly where we had left off. I managed to wrap my brain around at least a modicum of reality some of the time. More often than not, when I went into the club and paid for several dances, we talked more than anything.

She admitted her attraction to me, and acknowledged that, although she had no intention of making it what I wanted it to be, there was something there. In time it developed into something unique and unexplainable to others, something slightly more than customer/client yet not quite "companionship." "Amity" would falsely imply an absence of sensuality; and "friendship" would trivialize its very nature.

Still, neither of us being able to create a definition became irrelevant. We shared our secrets and hopes with each other. She told me stories of past relationships gone sour, about her family, her childhood, where she was from and other jobs she'd had. Not always so open, but I eventually learned the difference between when I was getting Sunrise and when I was getting Jennifer. We came to fulfill needs for each other. She made me feel special and desired and even loved; I made her feel like a person and not an object.

Unhappy in her relationship, I catered to her emotionally in a way her boyfriend did not. Many things passed between us in those moments that have no words, and once in discussing the nature of whatever this thing was we had, she said to me, "I don't know how to explain it, but part of it is just the way you look at me."

There were definitely moments of intimacy as we went along, and even real sexual desire that was mutual. She told me things without saying them, and voiced other things like, "I'm sure you can tell the difference between when it's real and when it isn't." I was right when I thought she was sometimes relieved to see me—she expressed gratitude for having something between us that allowed her to be herself, sometimes even vulnerable. After catering to men and their egos for hours, it was a welcome change to be with me.

We took up very limited e-mail correspondence but still, no matter how much I asked, there were two things she would never do: 1) see me outside the club, and 2) kiss me. My continuing to ask every once in a while was simply part of our dynamic; she now knew me well enough to know I was not dangerous or crazy, just a garden variety alcoholic. This "thing" we had just became a constant in my life.

Then something unexpected happened. She called me at home one day. I was working third shift then, so I was sleeping and it was the middle of the afternoon. I did lose that job I had and now lived in a basement apartment I could barely afford and I'd gotten a job with a security company. The ringing of the phone woke me and I let the machine pick up. Much to my surprise, it was her voice on the other end of the line. She was leaving me a message about a cat gym of all things. I interrupted her by picking up.

"Hello?"

"Angela, its Sunrise."

"I can't believe you're on the other end of my phone."

"Well, believe it. So listen, I'm cleaning some stuff out of my house and I know you have cats. I've got this cat gym plaything. I thought maybe you'd want it?"

"Sure. I'll take it off your hands. My cats love that kind of stuff."

"Where did you say you lived on Church Street? I want to drop it off."

She wanted to come to my house? What the fuck was happening? Was I dreaming? I gave her directions, got out of bed, had a cup of coffee and my first of many narcotic doses of the day, and waited. I couldn't believe it. What would that look like? What would I say? How would I act? As much as I might have imagined it, I really had no idea how to engage with her anywhere but the club.

One thing was certain—I was going to have the opportunity to give her a very long, honest, and heartfelt letter I'd written to her just the night before. She'd recently been forthcoming about where she was at in her life, wanting to get out of the dancing business, and out of a relationship that wasn't working for her any longer. I had enough wits about me to know it wasn't because of me, but still I dared to dream. Just maybe I would have my chance at being with the love of my life—I always think it's the love of my life while I'm in it. I still had not accepted the "no" that was continually so obvious. But in light of the genuine friendship and affection we'd developed toward each other, I had at least come to accept a "maybe no" from the universe, for I had decided this was a woman I wanted in my life anyway, even if it wasn't as my lover.

The doorbell rang and I nearly jumped out of my skin. Here was my moment of truth. I answered the door and there she was, in jeans and a sweatshirt without any makeup, just like a normal human being. She was beautiful. I'd had the occasion to see her in civilian clothing a handful of times when I was planted on my barstool early, before the girls came on shift, but only for a moment or two. She asked, "Will you help me?"

For a moment I thought she meant in life, with love, or something deeply meaningful or profound, but then I realized she meant getting the cat gym out of her car and into my apartment. I followed her outside and moments later we were back inside. I offered beverages and the very quick tour of my humble bachelorette pad. She took a glass of water and followed me through my three rooms, practically running out of my bedroom before I had the chance to engage her in small talk in such a provocative location. I asked if she could stay for a few minutes and we sat on the futon, one of my only pieces of furniture. All I could hear was the inside of my own head, repeating over and over, "I can't believe she's here, in my house."

I have no idea what we talked about but time moved at lightning speed and I could tell she had absolutely no intention of staying for more than 15 minutes total, so I had to act fast. That was easy, since I had a substantial amount of methamphetamines cruising through my bloodstream.

"I have something for you. And I have something to tell you...Jennifer."

She looked at me only slightly surprised. I had been unable to find the right moment to tell her I knew her real identity until then. I told her about Barbie and my adventurous night months ago. She laughed at my story—she always laughed at my stories, and didn't seem bothered by the fact I called her by name. It seemed appropriate since we were sitting in my house and we'd known each other for about 8 months.

I gave her the letter I'd written the night before and there was no conversation about it—my writing her letters was not new, but I had cut back severely on the frequency with which I did. She slipped the letter into her sweatshirt pocket and promised to read it later. Then she was saying goodbye and I was walking her to the door. I escorted her to her car, stole a quick hug, and watched her drive away.

That was it. The whole event couldn't have lasted more than 45 minutes from the start of her phone call to the end of her presence in my home. But, because I was addicted and obsessed, I assigned a whole lot of meaning to those 45 minutes I did not have to pay one red cent for.

Her coming to my house sent me directly back into the insanity of my "what ifs" and "just maybes" even worse than before. I re-launched my relentless campaign to get her out of the neon lights and into my life with all the fervor I'd had when we barely knew each other. But it was never enough, I was never satisfied, and I would never quit. That became glaringly obvious and led directly into another confrontation, except this time, I didn't get "the talk." I got an e-mail.

She wrote, "I have fears, HUGE fears that you still don't understand I cannot take this thing we have in a direction it is not going. I like you and I'm your friend but your behavior is unacceptable. I understand if you hate me and don't want to get dances from me anymore…"

On and on it went. Whatever the equivalent of a stripper you're not actually having a relationship with breaking up with you is, I'm pretty sure it looked a lot like this. I was enraged, all over again, right back where I'd started, hating myself for being crazy, because surely I was crazy if I ever actually believed we'd get together. I wrote her back, apologizing profusely and underhandedly throwing blame and guilt her way at the same time. Leaving the door open, because I always do, I wrote that I was open to further discussion because she had said the same. Then she called me.

Of course my first defense was the day she'd come to my house, what was that all about? She said, "You know, sometimes it feels good to be bad."

I did understand that. She was likely pissed off at her boyfriend and simply thought, "Fine, fuck you, I'm going to spend some time with someone I know who appreciates and adores me." She was human and I could forgive that, plus she said she was sorry and I knew she meant it.

Never once had she ever professed this was my entire fault and I admired her for that because it would have been easy to play it that way. Jennifer really was a person with solid values and even morals, which are what enabled me to fall in love with her in the first place. The more she tried to be honest and do the right thing, the more I was attached to her actual character. She had a lot of qualities I believed I wanted in a partner.

We went round and round for a while on the phone. Finally, I just flat out asked the question I was so afraid to ask. "Isn't it possible Jennifer, that you do have feelings for me?"

She hesitated, then said, "No. I really don't think I do."

And there it was, in black and white. Instead of facing that head-on like a grown-up, my brain immediately formulated this equation—"I really don't think so" does not equal, "Absolutely, positively, without a shadow of a doubt." That allowed my obsessive, addictive thinking to rationalize and justify there was some small sliver of hope for me to cling to.

However, that didn't happen on a conscious level. My consciousness acknowledged what she was saying, and that led to my ever familiar self-loathing. Apologetically and somewhat gracefully, I let her off the phone, leaving myself alone in my house and wide open for all sorts of self punishment and torture, and then, inevitably, back on the search for oblivion and escape.

I didn't see Jennie for a long time after that. My guilt and shame kept me away from the club, and my desire for destruction kept me occupied with more drugs and alcohol than ever. I'm not sure how long my life was lived in this condition, for much of it I cannot recall, and I'm actually quite grateful for that. Finding women to save me emotionally through sex and relationship was all but abandoned. My mission became singularly focused—not to feel better, but to feel nothing at all.

Through a profound series of unanticipated events, I got clean and sober. As a result, I began learning a great deal about my own unavailability and uncertainty, albeit mine was not about sexual or romantic orientation. What I came to know during my relationship with Jennifer was I am an addict and alcoholic. Anyone in recovery will tell you, ultimately, alcohol is not the alcoholic's problem. The real dilemma is how we've lived life, an inability to cope with reality, a constant searching for someone or something to fill a void, to fix ourselves, to be comfortable in our own skin. It's taken me years to comprehend how much my relationships with women—gay, straight, and bisexual alike—have to do with these great facts about addiction. That is not to say some of my dynamics have nothing to do with my alcoholism. It's nearly impossible to compartmentalize dysfunctionality.

Eventually, having gotten my bearings and a strong basis of support, I went back to the club. I found a handful of guys in the fellowship who had been sober a long time and still frequented the strip club, having traded one addiction for another. I judged them, but of course put myself in a different category. What do you think the odds are that being a sober alcoholic in a strip club actually led me to a) my first sponsor, b) my next lover, and c) the closest thing I'd had to a therapist in ten years? Well, that's what happened.

My relationship with Jennie continued along the same lines as it had always been, except now there was a new reality to it. Life clean and sober is very different, and it actually aided in our intimacy—she was really her and I was really me. To my surprise, I discovered Jennifer herself had spent some time in a 12-step program many years before. Although it "didn't take" for her, she remembered a lot of what she had learned—about herself, about addiction, about life. It became a habit of hers to tease me with the slogans she remembered when I would come in for dances. She would say, "One is too many and a thousand never enough?" Or, knowing all too well that I would, she'd occasionally say, "Keep coming back!" as I was leaving. It was endearing in a somewhat twisted way.

"Working a program," as recovering people call it, I tried to practice what I had learned about surrender and acceptance when it came to her. Still wanting very much to have an actual partnership, I acknowledged that was very unlikely. Yet, we still had something special, something I would come to hold very dear to my heart. Jennifer became emboldened to a point where she told me the truth about me, encouraged by my willingness to grow and become a better person. She really helped me.

If up until then I had any doubts she actually cared for me, they continued to dissipate the longer we knew each other. One fine example was after I'd returned from a trip to Cincinnati for a convention. I'd developed a long-distance crush on someone there, who was 100% lesbian, and during my visit it became clear she was not interested in me.

Feeling wounded and rejected, I went to the club with my tail between my legs to seek my usual comfort. Whining in that self-centered, self-pitying way, I played the victim to Jennifer. She said to me, "You know what? I could stroke your ego all night long, that's what I get paid to do…but, for some reason, I refuse to do it for you. If you want self-esteem, go volunteer at the animal shelter, or the nursing home. Don't come in here."

She was not afraid to call me out on bullshit, and I loved her for it. What a strange relationship to attempt to describe to others. I took much criticism for it from my friends who equated strip club/stripper with "non-sober behavior." Maybe it was. But it was what I needed at the time.

I came to understand the nature of my thinking, its cyclical nature, and as a result would vacillate between seeing her frequently and not seeing her for months. When things were good and I had other hobbies and activities to be involved in and focus on, I felt like I didn't need her. But whenever I had a new romantic interest fall through, and they always did, I would return to my comfort zone.

For two years running, she was the closest thing I had to a girlfriend, strange as it might sound. I would return to the same Jennifer-and-me fantasy again and again. Eventually I had to admit I used my relationship with her to change how I felt about myself, which was the exact same thing I'd done with drugs and alcohol my whole life. Still, more often than not, this acting out behavior was still presumably better than the alternative, plus it did have a certain level of basis in reality. We did like each other and there was genuine affection, care, and concern for each other.

The only other time we saw each other outside those four walls was when she had a tragedy of her own occur. I was on one of my hiatuses, so I had no idea what was happening in her world. Out of the blue, she e-mailed me at work one morning with a subject line that said, "need u, help." The body of the text said only, "I was hoping I could talk to you about some things, and you know how hard it is for me to ask in the first place because I wouldn't want you to turn this into something it isn't."

Given our history, she was entitled to that. I e-mailed her back and said, "Jennifer, I'm your friend. And whatever it is, I'm here for you. I promise to not try and take advantage of your vulnerability, I only want to help you, I care about you." And I actually meant it.

Ten minutes later, she called me at work and we made arrangements to meet for lunch to talk face to face. Now, I meant what I said to her, but she was still the current love of my life so I can't say waiting in that diner that day didn't have a certain amount of rapid heart racing anticipation. It did. But I was a sober person now, trying to live right and act right and be less self-consumed, before she got there I actually prayed for the willingness to do the right thing, and to show compassion for this other, obviously scared human being who came to me for help.

When she arrived, we had a quick round of small talk, ordered our lunch, and smoked a cigarette. Then she handed me a whole sheaf of papers printed out from her e-mail account. They were of the love letter variety, and it was clear whoever's voice this was came from a person very taken with her, and for reasons of their own was a little scared about it but couldn't manage to stay away from her for very long. I skimmed through most of what she'd handed me, wondering why I was given this to read in the first place. I asked, "This happens to you a lot, doesn't it?" which was, of course, an underhanded way of highlighting my own feelings for her that were never returned, and I immediately felt ashamed and sorry.

She told me the whole story about her and this man, who had begun his journey with her as a customer, just as I had. But apparently her connection with him was on a much deeper level, and she was falling for him too. Jennie was still in the same relationship she'd been in when I met her and, apparently, was still equally unhappy, if not more so, given she did have feelings for the writer of the letters I'd just read. I still wasn't sure what it was she needed my help with—surely I was not the best candidate she knew to go to for relationship advice. I knew that despite being a sociable person, she was mostly introverted and truthfully didn't have a host of close friends, particularly women friends. And I did know her—very well, I believed—so perhaps she just wanted friendly advice on what seemed like a mess, since she was involved with someone and, apparently, so was he.

While I was analyzing and decoding, I looked up at her and she was crying. I'd never seen her cry and it was heartbreaking to watch. I mean, I had deep love for this woman and would never want her to be in pain, ever. But life is life, and there we were, in real life dealing with a real problem and discussing it over lunch just like two normal people. To anyone else we must have looked like friends. Were we? As I looked at her across the table and held her hand while she cried, all I could think was, "Wow. How did this happen? Here is a person who, at one time, I was capable of stalking, and now, here we are having lunch and she's crying and coming to me for help."

Then it dawned on me—oh, my God, she actually trusts me. I had become a trustworthy person, of all things. Huh.

An addict/alcoholic in recovery from their disease is still self-centered. I'd been totally focused on my own thought process instead of being present for her, like I was supposed to. Luckily she was too upset to notice, so it was good I had. I put my focus back on her, still unsure what it was she needed from me. Then she told me this man had died of a heart attack just days ago. Now, I'm as codependent as they come, but for that I had no fix, no solution. I didn't have a clue what to say to her. She explained he was married, and right now her biggest concern was the man's wife, for how would she feel if she discovered all the e-mails and voice-mails and text messages that had passed between them?

It said volumes about what a good person Jennifer really was that this was her primary worry. She also explained where I fit in to all of this. She obviously couldn't talk to her boyfriend about what was happening, and the few friends she did have mostly worked at the same club as her, and this man had been a client in the beginning. Jennifer had a reputation for having excellent boundaries—I was certainly proof of that—and never mixing business with pleasure. I was the only person she had to talk to.

I was grateful for that. Finally, there was something I could do for her, instead of the other way around.

I told her exactly what I thought, and said the same exact things I would have said to anyone else in her position. The bottom line was that, although her feelings for this man were undoubtedly genuine, her reaction to the loss was about more than him. This was a turning point for her—tragedy is often a time of great reflection, for us to really take stock of where we're at and what we want out of this life before it is too late. I was as supportive as I knew how to be, and I was honest about what I believed based on my knowledge of her. For perhaps the first time, I was a good friend to her.

Lunch was a good idea because I had to go back to work.

Any other time I'd have stayed with her, or tried to anyway, all day long. I walked her to her car and told her I was always available to her, no matter what, only ever a phone call or e-mail away, just like today. She thanked me and hugged me, and I watched her drive away.

We didn't speak of this situation she was in except once or twice after that when she was sad and told me she missed him. One night, totally out-of-character for her, while I was getting dances, she broke down and cried on my shoulder. What a beautiful role-reversal. I was overjoyed I had become someone worthy of someone else's vulnerability and trust, particularly of someone I loved.

Inevitably, as I stayed sober, hanging out in a strip club became less and less desirable for me. I still wanted to see Jennifer, but became less willing to concede to only doing that on her terms. After almost four years of engaging in this sort of but sort of not relationship/friendship, I had to walk away. Almost for old time's sake, I tried one last time to convince her how beneficial a friendship outside the club would be.

She refused, mostly out of loyalty to her boyfriend, knowing if the roles were reversed, she would not be comfortable with him casually going out for pizza with a woman who was once completely obsessed with him and paid him for services that, in all reality, were sexual in nature. Her refusal of me still hurt, and still felt like rejection, but I understood. More importantly, this was something I had to do for myself if I wanted to continue to grow.

Giving her up was one of the most difficult things I'd ever done. Attachment and addiction to people are far greater to overcome than any substance. To say it was a struggle would be a huge understatement. But I got though it, and have been through much harder life challenges since.

I miss her sometimes and wonder if she ever thinks about me. Sometimes I still believed that, at some point, she actually did consider being with me, but she was unsure. But if you asked me today how she really felt about me during all that time, it is I who remains uncertain.

Chapter 5: Terry
"We're already doing it."

WHEN I WAS seventeen and in that relationship with my first girlfriend, the evil cheating one, an adult person in my life suggested I read *Codependent No More*. Already having a well-established core belief that the answer to everything can always be found in books, I dutifully marched into the bookstore and bought a copy. I don't recall reading it in its entirety. To me it was about how to resolve and/or handle having a relationship with an alcoholic, which, ironically, meant zero to me at the time. I skimmed through the book, trying to understand why this title had been suggested to me.

Then I came across chapter four, "Codependent Characteristics." I didn't really see myself in the care-taking list that was not particularly part of my dynamic in relationships, yet. But I read on about low self-worth, denial, obsession, dependency, and controlling behavior, and I thought, "Hmm…yes, yes, some of this is sounding very familiar…"

In the almost twenty years since then, I can't tell you how many times I have returned to this book, seeing more and more and more of myself and my relationships, and not just romantic ones either. When I was newly sober, the blinding reality of these issues came to pass with my first "unsure" in recovery.

Getting clean, going to meetings, and changing everything about my life was a frightening endeavor, but one I was dedicated to doing. One of the reasons twelve-step programs work is because of the people waiting for you on the other end, ready to help you learn how to live life. One of those people, unbeknownst to me, was going to be my next lesson in blurring the lines between sexuality, friendship, and intimacy.

They tell you to get phone numbers and call people if you want to stay sober. Of course, I called only women, and women I found attractive at that—not an uncommon phenomenon, by the way. After my first week of meetings, I called Terry. She was six months clean and, to me, that was something to be worshiped. She knew everything there was to know, she knew every person at every meeting and could quote the literature verbatim, and seemed only interested in helping me not use drugs or alcohol and get connected with this new family of sorts. I followed her everywhere.

It didn't take me long to understand she was hooked up with a guy we knew and, for some reason, I found this terribly distressful and felt rejected. I didn't even think I liked her *like that* initially, but how else could I explain my feelings of disappointment every time she was unavailable to me?

But my disappointment didn't last long. A couple of months after we knew each other, she came to me with an elaborate sob story about living with her brother and his new intensely Christian wife, and that was not at all working out. She was sad, victimized, didn't know what to do or where she was going to go. So I let her move in with me.

I was often lonely, so having someone there, and someone I liked on top of that, did me a lot of good. However, I didn't like the frequency with which my phone rang and it was never for me. I didn't like the dishes in the sink, what little rent she was paying being late, the odd hours she kept, or her alarming lack of employment. But when she was there, and we were having those deep, intimate, heartfelt conversations long into the night, I forgot all of those other things. I was being taught to accept other people for who they were, and to look for people who accepted me exactly as I was, with all of my flaws and insecurities. This was her gift to me. I grew to trust her and, little by little, let her into my heart, telling her my deepest secrets and fears.

Terry had many of the hallmark traits of the unsure. She had a sordid sexual history that revolved around her drug use and, not surprisingly, had had affairs with women. An addict will go anywhere to get what they need, even if it goes against the grain of who they are at their core. She had a trauma dynamic and a history of abuse, which fed into my savior complex with her and other women like her. Terry also had a very hardened exterior but a soft and tender heart, which led me to believe that, because she let me see the vulnerable side of her, I was special, a chosen one. Things reached a point where anytime I showed up at a social function without her, people would ask me, "Where's Terry?" In a distorted perception, this made me feel like we were a couple, albeit we were not romantically involved.

I noticed the now familiar progression of affection in our relationship. There was something slightly abnormal about the level of touching between two people who were, for all intents and purposes, only friends. Of course, I liked it, so instead of raising an issue or setting clear and healthy boundaries (which I had no idea how to do), I just let it go on, inevitably spurring us toward something more.

One night I was in bed listening to Terry argue with an ex-boyfriend back in her hometown. I don't really recall what it was about, except the now-clean addict's challenge of cutting old using and drinking buddies out of their current lives. She finally hung up on him, then I heard her crying. I called out to her, summoning her to my bed. We had slept in the same bed together on occasion before, for comfort, nurturing, and relief from loneliness, a bit of cuddling here and there, totally inno-cent. But this particular night was about to change everything.

I held her in my arms while she cried and stroked her hair. For what seemed like a long time, neither of us said anything at all. Then, without a word, she turned to me and kissed me.

That was the first time I'd been kissed in a very long time, so immediately the floodgates were opened—emotionally, sexu-ally, and every other kind of arousal there is. She climbed on top of me, kissed me some more, whispered my name. She paused for only a moment, then took off her shirt.

In my one, weak attempt to do the right thing, I said, "You know, this is probably a bad idea."

I distinctly remember the sound of her breathing in that moment, and the soft *swoosh* the sound her shirt made as it hit my tile floor. She looked me in the eye and said, "We're already doing it."

First time sober sex is an event. A lot of things went on in my head that had very little to do with Terry, but everything to do with me and my own past, my recent escapades at the strip club with Jennifer, my overwhelming fear of being alone and having an utter inability to take care of myself. Program-speak cautions people in recovery against sex and relationships in early sobriety because we are prone to use that person, act, or rela-tionship in the same manner—compulsively, addictively, as a shield against the reality of our own lives.

Of course, none of *this* occurred to me. I also completely chose to ignore the fact Terry had had sex with a man only a few nights before in my own living room while I slept, and God only knew how many men before that. I still liked to hide be-hind the "lesbians are not at risk" myth, even though I knew better. Not once did it occur to me I might be being used or taken advantage of, that this woman was in my bed partially because I'd given her a place to live and she felt like she owed me that much.

No, none of these thought processes would override the

immediate need to have an orgasm and cause someone else to do the same. I believed this was the measure of my own self-worth.

After an extended make-out session, she tried to maneuver our bodies to position me for oral sex. This is usually my first clue about someone's inherent heterosexuality. Straight women, just like straight men, always want to go for oral sex first because they make the false assumption that, simply by definition of being a lesbian, that is what I want. As if this sexual act is all lesbians ever engage in, as if we have no imagination whatsoever, or we all live up to the standard pornographic stereotype. Although I enjoy oral sex as much as the next person, I also long for connectedness and intimacy, which means I prefer to be close to my lover, feel her breath on my skin, kissing, all things made impossible when I'm "up here" and she's "down there." So I surprised her by steering her away from that, concentrating instead on what she and I could both do with hips and hands rather than mouth and tongue.

I couldn't make her come, which frustrated me. I assumed that was about my lack of ability, which I once had great confidence in. Again, there was that self-pitying type of self-centeredness. It just *had* to be about me. She assured me repeatedly it wasn't, but I didn't believe her. I fell asleep next to her, embarrassed and ashamed. We were far closer to intimacy and true friendship there, lying side by side, then we had been when we attempted to escape the harsh reality of ourselves through each other's bodies.

The next few days and weeks were awkward at best. I had no idea how to have a casual sexual relationship with someone I cared about, let alone someone living with me. I had far too many expectations, and one by one they were crushed as Terry spun further and further toward a relapse, and I became wrapped tighter and tighter in the grips of codependency. Within two weeks she'd moved out of my place and in with a man in the program who, of course, also wanted to be with her. The more I attempted to get close to her, the further away she got, which only led to incredible self-criticism and torture. I thought I'd chased her out of my life by being too needy, by failing to separate sex from emotion, and a thousand other things I assumed I'd done wrong. In reality, none of what happened to Terry after that had one bit to do with me.

As I grew and learned about my relationship dynamics, I got over whatever romantic idealism permeated that relationship. What I realized was how truly connected we were—this had never been about sex or attraction, Terry was the best friend I'd always wanted as a little girl. But where I was growing, she was tumbling backward from where she came and, although I no longer had the desire to sleep with her, I wanted more than ever to save her.

She'd grown fond of avoiding me most of the time, and when we ran into each other at a convention, she told me we had to talk. Guilt, shame, it's all my fault, etc., etc.—the tape played over and over. When we finally had a moment alone, she said, "Look, this whole you lusting after me thing isn't working for me."

Of course, that triggered the tape to play louder. Terry did a grown up thing, though, at least to a point—she owned up to her own responsibility in what had happened between us. She was smart enough to know that, aside from our obvious dysfunction, we did have a legitimate friendship, and I loved her outside of a romantic context. We talked for a long time. She said up until then she'd been a coward, and apologized for not coming to me sooner to lay her cards on the table. Finally, she spoke the words that, by now, I'd become accustomed to. "I love you—you are one of my best friends. But I'm not gay."

And there it was. Again.

We rebuilt after that. However, try as we might, a relationship built on unhealthiness will remain unhealthy until both parties make an effort to actually become healthier themselves. I tried to do that, but whenever it came to her, I had no defenses, and no boundaries. I knew she was on her way back to active drug use, and I was powerless to do anything to stop her. This was heartbreaking for me, since this was the person who taught *me* how to stay clean and sober. My life became a constant emotional battle and I couldn't let go no matter how hard I tried. She would disappear for weeks at a time, and I kept waiting for the phone call that would tell me she was dead. That call never came, but one nearly as bad finally did.

After simply praying she would find her way and trying to detach gently, I found some peace. She and her partner, Dave, were missing again, or in jail, or on the road, or God knew what. They came in and out of sobriety so often, it just became something I got used to. After about a year of this, I was at home when the phone rang and it was Terry on the other end. She would not tell me what happened, only that she was in the ER and asked me to come to her.

When I got to the ER, I completely expected to find Dave, along with any number of other people we knew in common. No one was there. Of all the contacts she had, she called only me. She looked like she'd been to hell and back—bruised, hollow, unclean, unkempt. For all of that, though, to me she looked innocent, a victim of the disease of addiction, which I'd come to personify and hate with a passion. I pushed her hair away her face and kissed her on the forehead, saying nothing. She looked at me and started to cry. "I overdosed on heroin," she stated matter-of-factly.

My reaction wasn't one of surprise. I don't quite know what it was. Sobriety itself was still relatively new, but being in the ER because someone you loved had overdosed was entirely unknown territory. I guess what I felt was the first word I learned the true meaning of in recovery—powerless. I couldn't save her or otherwise help her. She would not stop until she was ready to…or until she was dead. This was a fact. I had truly let go of her and my relationship with her when my sponsor had said to me quite plainly, "You will enable her right into the grave."

So now what?

The hospital released her to me when she was stable. I must have appeared safe, with my Narcotics Anonymous Basic Text in my hand and my recovery speak. They thought I knew something they didn't. In fact I did—I knew things about addiction only an addict can truly know. The hospital staff, baffled by Terry and dozens like her, foolishly assumed whatever I knew would keep her from using again.

I knew it wouldn't. But I also knew I could keep her from that for one night if I kept her with me, so I brought her home. She had told me Dave was on the run. He had been the one to call an ambulance, but knew the police would arrive with the paramedics, so he'd disappeared from the scene once he saw she was breathing. There were several warrants out for his arrest, but there weren't for her—at least, not yet.

I said nothing all the way home. What could I have said? I cried while I drove, thanked God she hadn't died, and silently prayed for guidance about what to do next. I helped her shower, put her in clean sweatpants and a T-shirt, made her soup and crackers. We said very little, other than her relaying what she remembered of the evening's events, which I didn't particularly want to hear. I don't know what they put into you to get heroin out, but whatever it is, it's probably also narcotic. Terry was still foggy, unclear, not quite away but not quite there.

There was nothing else to do but go to bed, together. I held her while she cried. In my own sickness I was still attracted to her which, under those circumstances, brought up in me an incredible amount of guilt and shame. I still operated from a belief deep within that if I could just love her enough or in the right way, as no one else had, then I could fix her. I loved her deeply, like a sister, but because we'd had sex once, my signals would get all confused, having lived a life with no real sense of what intimacy meant.

Terry and I had developed a theory a while back that we had shared at least one, if not many, past lives. The feeling is hard to describe, and one I've only had with a handful of people—a deep sense of connectedness that must certainly extend beyond the current state of being in each other's lives. I had not grown enough to know how to put such deep emotion in its proper place, and neither had she.

She began to stroke me, my body, my face, in a way that signaled sexual desire, not friendly sisterly admiration. I should have stopped her—she wasn't even fully sober—but I didn't. Making love to her was the only way I knew how to communicate my caring, not knowing the difference between passion and compassion. It wasn't appropriate, but even if our heads and hearts couldn't recognize that, our bodies did, and the sexuality of what we were doing quickly gave way to more crying and more appropriate, comforting caresses, given the situation. I held her until she fell asleep, my tears soaking into her long black hair, and I knew when I came home from work the next day, she'd be gone again.

She was. There was absolutely nothing I could do, except what I'd already done, which was to try and emotionally prepare myself for coming home to an empty house. At least addicts are predictable. I called my sponsor and cried, going through the whole cycle of emotions all over again. They say insanity is repeating the same mistakes over and over and expecting different results. By that standard, then, I had driven myself insane. Again.

She played with me for the next several weeks and I allowed it. She convinced me Dave was essentially holding her captive, she couldn't leave, couldn't break free—if she tried to quit using, he'd quite likely kill her. I had already watched him find her and retrieve her from meetings in the past; he'd shown up at my own house a dozen times when he couldn't find her anywhere else.

Still, I knew the game. Would he look for her? Yes. Would he actually kill her, or even attempt to try and harm her physically? I thought not. Just knowing each of them, their personalities, and sheer physical stamina, Terry could have pinned Dave to the floor in a few quick moves and he wouldn't have known what hit him.

When my life was unmanageable enough and I was in enough pain, I knew I had to take some drastic action if I didn't want to continue to be sucked back into this cycle. I had to say no to her, to turn her away; otherwise, she would keep coming back and I would never move on.

She called me at work one afternoon and asked me to come get her from where she was staying with Dave. I left work, drove over there, only to discover she was nowhere to be found and, instead, found myself being spoken to by Dave, who said everything was fine and I could go away now, thank you.

That was my last straw. I drove home and called my friend Sandy, hysterical, knowing Terry would be turning up on my doorstep any minute. I said, "I don't know if I can say no to her."

Sandy, gratefully a bit codependent herself, said, "Do you need me to come over and say it for you?"

I didn't know, but it would sure help if she were there, so she came over and waited with me while I continued to break down. True to form, within a half hour, Terry was knocking on my door.

I let her in, and she was surprised to see Sandy there, but quickly recovered from feeling threatened and launched into her latest fabrication about why she hadn't show up at the door when I bolted out of work and went over there. Sandy jumped in and wasn't very reserved about telling Terry exactly what she thought of her, based only on what little, one-sided information she had from me. Sandy accused her of being a self centered addict who thought of no one but herself, and couldn't she see what she was doing to me?

Terry had the audacity to glare at me with a look that said, "Are you going to just sit there and let her talk to me that way?"

It was a three-way codependent split—I wanted to protect Terry from Sandy, Sandy wanted to protect me from Terry, and I, of course, had slept with one of them and *wanted* to sleep with the other so I was torn. It was so dysfunctional, you could practically have imagined it on a big screen, complete with a dramatic instrumental score in the background.

I asked Terry where she planned on staying, and she said what I knew she would: "I figured I'd stay here."

Sandy stared at me, challenging me to do the right thing for myself. If she hadn't been there, I don't know I would have. I took a deep breath and said, "Terry, I love you. You know I do. But I can't let you stay here."

Without a word, she gathered her things and walked out. I followed her into the hallway and made a blubbering attempt to explain this was best for both of us, that I wasn't helping her by rescuing her all the time.

She didn't want to hear it and wouldn't let me touch her. "I'll see you around, Ang." And she was gone again.

The only thing that made the whole episode bearable was I knew I would walk back into my apartment and be comforted by another woman I was addicted to. I got what I wanted from Sandy—she held me while I cried and completely agreed with me that, when it came to Terry, I had been a victim. She allowed me to live in my own delusion.

I didn't see Terry for many months after that. She and Dave would disappear to another state and come back when they ran out of money. They'd hang around meetings just to swindle enough and then be gone again. A real modern day Bonnie and Clyde, except obviously strung out most of the time. For a while whenever they turned up somewhere I was, it induced a full-on panic attack and I'd have to leave immediately. Sometimes she would follow me outside and beg me to talk to her. She'd say, "I love you," and I'd argue, "Don't say that because you don't know what it means."

But I was growing, changing, my threshold limits for chaos and drama lowering. Just as I'd learned to deal with their sporadic appearances and my middle of the night driving the streets of our city looking for her among the prostitutes ceased completely, Terry and Dave disappeared altogether. Within a year I stopped hearing any mention of their names or their where-abouts on the rumor mill.

I went on with my life and my own sobriety, but never for-got her completely. Most people assumed at least one of them had died and the other couldn't be far behind. I didn't believe that. I didn't care if he was dead, I hated him, resented him, and blamed him. Even though I knew she was a willing participant, without him she might have stood half a chance. I knew from watching so many others that two using addicts who were also emotionally and sexually intertwined didn't have a prayer.

Yet somewhere deep within my heart, maybe even my soul, I had a deep understanding that, if she were dead, I would just *know*. I lived a long time with that belief deep at my core.

Shortly before my four-year sobriety anniversary, I took a job as an addictions counselor in the local outpatient treatment agency. Working in that field, I was suddenly privy to a lot of local law enforcement and social services information I hadn't had access to before, and if I myself wasn't privy, someone above me was. One day, a very good friend and confidante, who had stood by my side through the "Terry experience," came into my office and closed the door behind her. "I have something to tell you. It's big."

I assumed it was about one of my clients—as you can imag-ine, working in treatment usually comes with much more bad news than good. Instead, she said, "Terry's in county lockup." She waited a minute and asked, "Are you okay?"

I was and I was not. I hadn't thought about Terry on a con-scious level in a long time. I'd been at peace with the past we had, the inappropriate sexual relationship, and whatever guilt and shame I associated with the whole ball of wax. Good men-toring over the years, and good therapy, had taught me my rela-tionship with Terry and what ensued after that in watching her self-destruct wasn't devastating because I was ever *in* love with her. It was distressing because I loved her, *really* loved her, as if she'd been my own sister. There was a very child-like innocence about our intimacy that had come to mean a great deal to me in a very nostalgic way—she'd been my best friend far more than she had my lover. The very absence of her allowed my feelings to change into something far more real and, therefore, far more painful.

I sat with the information for about a week, really considering whether I wanted to go visit her, and what that might mean for me. I thought about how many people I had come into contact with who'd been incarcerated, and one part of their story was always the same—either they were devastated by no one writing or visiting, or they were eternally grateful to the ones who did when they thought there was no one left who cared.

So I went.

We came from very different places in our addiction, and I'd never set foot inside a law enforcement institution in my life. I called ahead to the jail and asked a lot of questions to make sure I could visit even though I wasn't family. There was no way to let her know ahead of time I was coming. This was an entirely new experience for me, and I kept thinking, "If I'm this scared, wonder what it must be like to actually be the prisoner?"

That thought got me through the door. I signed a form, showed my driver's license, and waited with all the other visitors. I was the only one who looked terrified.

When I went into the little glass booth, she did not look the least bit surprised to see me. I hid my shock at how thin she was, how hollow, but I knew immediately I had done the right thing. Whatever bond we had was still there, and it wasn't lust, it wasn't codependent, it wasn't dysfunctional. It was real, and I was moved to tears both because I was so happy she was still alive and had another chance to change, and because I was grateful my own addiction had not taken me where she had been.

Twenty minutes is not a very long time to spend with someone you care deeply about. What happened in those twenty minutes, though, was worth my entire life up until that moment. For the first time ever, I was having a brand new relationship evolve out of misguided sexual energy and romantic longing. I finally had an unsure who actually belonged in my life under a different label—*friend*. So, for a change, I became a friend myself.

Chapter 6: Sandy
"Why do we have to have a label?"

I WANTED SANDY from the moment I met her. Though, given it was in the strip club, that's hardly remarkable. What *is* remarkable is it actually happened.

Unlike Jennifer/Sunrise, Sandy was not quite as good at professional versus personal boundaries. It was a totally ordinary occurrence for her to hang out with, befriend, or even occasionally date people she originally met as customers. I met Sandy during one of my emotional hiatuses away from Jennifer, and after only a few dances and conversations spread out over a couple of weeks, I had convinced her I was the victimized lonely girl I wanted everyone to see. We struck up an intensely emotional friendship, based on my now familiar M.O. that, if I could make myself emotionally indispensable to a woman, there might be the slightest chance of someday turning the friendship into something else.

Sandy was very charismatic and I was immediately enraptured. She found me intriguing in the ways most bisexual women do, though I'm still not really sure how that is. Nevertheless, I had a new fantasy to build, so I went to work. Before long, I had written Sandy letters, burned her mixed CDs, spent endless hours bearing my soul, all in spite of the fact she was in a happily committed relationship with a man. I figured if I could get a woman to meet my emotional needs, a sexual or even romantic relationship was not entirely necessary—I could take care of those components largely through masturbation and my own imagination. As long as I was "special" in some way, it didn't really matter which way that was.

To Sandy, I was special because at some point I had deemed her my new best friend and I hers. I lived with the secret knowledge she was getting some emotional needs fulfilled by me her boyfriend fell short on and, for me, starved for connection insatiably, that was enough.

Once, and only once, I almost kissed her. I had spent the night at her house, a "girls' night" with her and a few others— movies, junk food, facials, hair dying. In the morning when she came into the spare bedroom to wake me for work, she crawled into bed with me. We had done this before at my house. Again, I had found someone willing to engage in an entirely inappropriate level of affection for two women who were supposedly "just friends." For hours we would lie, cuddle, and talk. This time, for whatever reason, I was emboldened, and I leaned up to kiss her on the throat. She said my name, and before she could follow that with, "I can't," I was up and out the door. We never spoke about it.

After about a year of fantasizing about our someday relationship, I was crushed when she told me she was moving away with Brian. He was opening a tattoo parlor in his hometown with a couple of buddies. This did afford me, however, a new dramatic spin, so I added to my repertoire regular phone calls and e-mails lamenting our distance, and finding new and creative ways to keep her engaged. When she couldn't see me, I could get her to worry about me even more than she normally did. I would intentionally disappear from the radar for brief periods, only to return and weep uncontrollably on the phone, telling her I missed her and didn't know how I could possibly survive without her.

Part of this was true, as I was headlong into my alcohol and methamphetamine career shortly after she moved away. I wanted her to be the cure, the fix I needed to end my suffering, my self-destruction. After a particularly harrowing three day run and a near overdose, I decided it was time to go and see her, to profess my undying love and need for her once and for all.

I scored my drugs for the road, called and increased the limit on my credit card, booked a hotel for one night, and was on my way. In my delusion, if I could get Sandy to be with me, to love me enough, I could change this sorry excuse for a life I lived and turn things around. I did need her, and convinced myself I could quit everything I was doing for her, and only for her. But that weekend didn't go how I planned, not at all.

I drove nearly two hundred miles to still be "just friends." We spent some time together, and I dropped not-so-subtle sub-texts in our conversations about her being "the one," but our friendship went on very much as it always had. My drugs ran out and my exterior was cracking, and she knew. Before I got in my car and drove away that weekend, she kissed me on the cheek, looked into my eyes with a sadness I can remember to this day, and said, "I love you so much, but I can't help you. Please, please, get some help."

My help eventually came, but not for a good long while. In that time, after one too many desperate and pleading phone calls, I pushed Sandy beyond her capacity for compassion which, at the time, was greater than anyone I'd known. All other relationships to varying degrees of real friendship had faded away, and I was locked into a prison of my own making. She was all I had in the world, and that's far too much pressure for anyone to take. She finally did what most people would have done much earlier. She walked out of my life. It took me a long time to understand just how hard that had been for her to do.

As fate would have it, about nine months after I'd finally gotten my act together, Sandy and Brian broke up and she moved back to town. I heard this through the grapevine at the strip club, as she and I had no contact for some time—about a month after that weekend visit, I had finally conceded to her wishes and stopped trying to contact her. By the time she came back, I had learned quite a few distasteful things about myself, not the least of which was how unfairly I had treated her in my active addiction.

So when I heard she was back in town, I went looking to make some genuine amends. After all, if she hadn't turned her back to me, I might never have sought the help I needed. She had done me the most loving service I think anyone ever had up until that point—the very least I owed her was an apology.

Amazingly, Sandy and I were able to move beyond our brief history and pick up our friendship in very much the same way we'd left it. This re-ignition was, of course, complete with emotional and physical intimacy, with the subtext of my desire for her right below the surface. To prevent myself from making any passes at her, I kept reminding myself about Steven, the new boy on Sandy's block. She never could go very long without a boyfriend. I was pretty certain Steven was a new customer-turned-partner since she'd gone back to working at the club, but I didn't ask. Besides, I had a feeling Steven, being the rebound boyfriend, wouldn't last very long.

I went through a particularly rough patch with an ex-lover I'd also made amends to—this business of making amends is part of any twelve-step program—who showed up on my doorstep one night just as Sandy and I were leaving to meet friends for dinner.

This laid new groundwork for my setup of "needing" her, to protect me from this other "bad" woman who had hurt me. As a matter of fact, that night landed me the reward of Sandy once again cuddling with me in my bed. She even stayed all night and I had the joy of falling asleep in her arms for the first time.

My label of "best friend" took on new importance, and she became a cheerleader for my sobriety. That weekend I'd traveled to see her, now almost two years prior, she had thought I was going to die. The truth is, if I hadn't stopped abusing drugs and alcohol when I did, I quite likely would have. This implicit fact seemed to tie her more firmly to me—the fact she had almost lost me cemented her attachment. We did everything together, cooked dinner for each other, exchanged elaborate Christmas gifts, talked to each other everyday…it was like having a girlfriend without her actually being that.

By then this was something I had come to settle for regularly. I called it "having acceptance." It was clear to me she was not interested in me romantically, but that was okay because she still paid me a lot of attention. I denied the "maybe someday" fantasy to my very core, and actually convinced myself I had "let it go."

Perhaps I had. They say sometimes the minute you stop longing for something, it comes to you. That's exactly what happened with Sandy. We were out on a romantic evening (for me, anyway), visiting a tourist attraction popular around the holidays—the Dana Thomas house in Springfield. It's a Frank Lloyd Wright house built in the 1800s and every year they decorate it as it was then, complete with a luminary tour of the grounds. We'd planned it for weeks, and beforehand had an elegant dinner at a nearby restaurant.

All night had that "couple-feeling" and my little plans and designs were tugging at my head and heart. I forgot all about Steven, still sure he was just a temporary phase. It was a wonderful evening but, when it ended, I had a moment of clarity I was not expecting. Sandy was saying goodbye to me, preparing to leave, putting on her coat, and we were in my bedroom. She hugged me and, in a common move of mine, I pulled her onto my water bed. She giggled the way she always did, and joked with me for a little while, reiterating needing to get home. I feigned disappointment, our well rehearsed routine.

Just then, some minuscule speck of self-worth kicked in. There we were, in my bedroom, in my *bed* no less, with me on my back and her straddled across my midriff, and I thought, "You know what? If she doesn't want me in this moment, she's never going to."

After she left, I wrote about the experience, in case I needed to remind myself of the obvious conclusion I had finally come to.

This surrender of mine made our friendship a lot easier—she must have sensed that lack of pressure she'd always felt from me bubbling just below the surface. After all, we did thoroughly enjoy each other's company. I was free from my obsession, though I did still struggle with my actual physical attraction to her. I was not yet healthy enough to set better boundaries. Either way this was progress, and progress I did not take lightly on my self-improvement journey.

One night I dropped by her place unannounced, which was common for both of us. She was home and had a friend over. Within the first ten minutes I was there, I read the entire situation. When she let me in, I immediately saw the "Oh, thank GOD you're here" expression. Shortly thereafter, I put together why.

The friend was a male friend, of course, which is mostly what Sandy had. It was obvious said friend (he was so insignificant I don't remember his name) had a not-so-hidden agenda and she, much to my delight, was clearly not interested. I had completely rained on his parade, and he was miffed I was there.

Ha! I thought, "Well, she might not be fucking me, but she doesn't want to fuck you, so I'm still better!" I might not have won out over Steven yet, but at least I was a higher priority than this jerk. As casually and, to my credit, as kindly as possible, I asked what they're plans were for the evening. Dude read his cues, made a few lame attempts to get both of us to go with him for a drink somewhere, then gave up and said he wanted to go stay at his friend's house. His entire pretense had been being kicked out by his girlfriend. I said, "Oh, okay. I'll drive you."

When we were walking down the stairs of Sandy's building, she whispered a quick "thank you" in my ear. I loved being the hero, particularly to her because she was, for the most part, fiercely independent, and didn't need a hero very often.

After we dropped him off, she told me the whole story of how they knew each other. They were kind of friends but she kept her distance because she didn't trust his motives. Ironically, I asked her to come and stay at my place for the night and she didn't question mine. Although, really, I didn't either, since I believed I had grown past all of that.

I was about to find out I hadn't.

We got some dinner, went back to my place, and crawled into bed together as per our standard operating procedure. I don't know what made that night different from any other when we'd taken the same actions. Either I had become very bold or she had become less guarded, or maybe a combination of the two. Or the stars lined up with Venus or some other astrological phenomenon or miracle shift in the universe.

Whatever it was, after a good hour and a half of intimate conversation and gentle caressing, I had the nerve to actually kiss her.

She kissed me back.

A lengthy, heated, marathon followed. No speaking, only kissing. After a while and a bit of repositioning, I sensed just the slightest bit of tension and hesitation. Any human being in my position, particularly *that* position, with a woman they had wanted for years, would have just pushed on ahead, knowing only a nudge was needed for complete coercion.

That is, any human being in their right mind. Instead, I stopped kissing and asked, "What's wrong?"

In my world, even sex could not possibly be complete or remotely fulfilling without a touch of drama.

She responded, "Nothing. I'm just deciding if I want to break the make out barrier."

I searched for the right words, knowing whatever I was

about to say would be crucial. Fear set in as my brain realized I had nothing. So I did the only possible next thing—I started kissing her again, more aggressively, and let my hands wander down her body just a little farther than I had before.

You know that moment with a lover when you know? A quick intake of breath, the feel of a racing heartbeat up against yours, that look between you that says, "Game on?" Well, Sandy looked deep into my eyes and said, "I don't want to hurt you."

I would discover much later that one sentence apparently absolved her of any wrongdoing from that moment forth. However, the truth is, even if I had known that, my response would have been the same, solely for the purposes of instant gratification. I whole-heartedly believed what I said in response. "I've wanted this for a long time. You're my best friend, and no matter what happens, it will all be okay." Game on.

Sex with Sandy was even better than I'd imagined it would be. She was direly sexy, playful, skilled and, above all, I felt completely at ease with her. I had no shame about my far less than athletic physique, even in the light of her body's perfection. I did have some minimal "performance anxiety"—Sandy had had many lovers, of both sexes, and I wasn't sure who I was being compared to, if at all.

It didn't occur to me until long after that night Sandy was the only woman I had ever had sex with who I'd had a friendship with first. Now, one could argue that was only because she didn't give into me sooner, but it was still a valid point that would lead to a greater emotional struggle later on. Either way, separate from other context, sex was sex, and sex was good, and I hadn't had sex since Terry. It was a powerful draw that did not calculate any sort of logical reasoning into the process.

If the sex was good, the sleeping was even better. I hadn't fallen asleep curled around a lover (and a non-addicted lover, at that) for a very, very long time. It was the most peaceful sleep I'd had in I don't know how long. I felt safe, cared for, loved. And, if you've read this far into my little book of relationships gone south, you already know that's my hook.

I awoke to the sound of my phone ringing. I answered it at my bedside and it was a friend in distress. Sandy was still sleeping, so I got up and went into the other room as I talked to my friend and made coffee. When it was ready, still on the phone, I walked back into the bedroom, brought Sandy a cup, and kissed her good morning. It was the most natural thing in the world. No weirdness, no shyness, no nothing. I had gratitude in the moment, which was rare for me.

My friend on the phone realized I was not alone and asked, "Who's there?"

"Sandy," was all I responded.

"Oh, my God. Did she spend the night?"

"Yes."

"Did you sleep with her?"

"Yes."

"Oh, my God, you have to call me later and tell me all about it!" My friends were painfully aware of my friendship with Sandy and my obsession about turning it into more.

I hung up the phone and crawled back under the covers. "Well, hi," she said, and kissed me. We cuddled for a little while, then I suggested a little post-coitus breakfast. We spent the morning together in blissful couple-dom.

But that perception wasn't entirely accurate. After I left her at her place and went home to study for a class I was taking, I reviewed all the information I thought was relevant. We were friends. We'd been through a lot together. Check. We'd had sex and it was great. Check. The next morning we were still friends and very much attracted to each other. Check. I knew Sandy was not the monogamy or commitment type. Check.

Wait, really? I'm just going to check that?

Yes. To the deepest core of my denial system, which was still very much intact, that knowledge got pushed down and buried along with my knowledge of Steven.

Although I had known about Steven for some time, it

didn't bother me because whenever she spoke of him, all she did was complain. I took comfort in comparing myself to him, and it was obvious to me I was fulfilling a role he was incapable of filling. I introduced Sandy to the phrase "emotionally unavailable" and she used it to describe Steven nearly every time she mentioned him.

Ironically, that phrase I was more than happy to assign to nearly anyone but myself. Years later someone would say to me, "Did it ever occur to you that you pursue these emotionally unavailable women because YOU yourself are unavailable?"

I had no idea, and it had certainly never occurred to me with Sandy, because I thought I was completely available to her. I always had been.

In any event, Sandy continued to see both of us (when I say "see," I mean have sex with) for the next couple of months. Every time I knew she could have been with him and chose to be with me it felt like victory, like I was *winning*. It never occurred to me I was, in a way, being used.

I knew about Steven, but he didn't know about me. He knew me, he knew we were friends, but that was all. I was the dirty little secret, and it wasn't the first time I'd been one. Instead of being bothered by that, I was proud of it. It fueled my ego and self-obsession. I became thoroughly convinced she would eventually realize she wanted to be with me and not him. With me and not with anyone else.

How does this happen with a woman who has told you time and time again she isn't looking for a long-term committed relationship? I think in this case it was because I read half her cues correctly and the other half incorrectly. As I would soon discover, Sandy *did* want a long-term committed relationship, complete with romance and falling head-over-heels in love. She just didn't want it with me.

For the first month or so I had myself convinced I was perfectly fine with things the way they were. I didn't admit I was fine with things *as long as* I got the outcome I wanted. It didn't take much longer than a month for my emotional life to be completely unmanageable, and for me to be utterly obsessed with said outcome. The fourth and last time we were together in bed, I incurred the non-monogamy faux pas. I said, "I love you," while we were having sex.

That was immediately followed by a deer-in-headlights look. She said it back, but I knew I'd made a terrible mistake. She didn't mean it the way I meant it, and I knew it. I'm not even sure I meant it that way but felt like I was supposed to. I mean, I *did* love her. But I had equated sex with falling in love for so long, I wasn't really sure what that was supposed to look like yet. I had not unlearned my fractured core beliefs about myself or relationships. That would take years and years and lots of therapy.

Sandy fed my "I'm winning" mindset. She would tell me Steven would come to the club, completely expecting her to come home with him. So smugly confident, he would say things like, "So what kind of eggs do you want for breakfast?" He was baffled every time she told him she had other plans. I was *always* the other plans.

She seemed to enjoy telling me these things while lying in my arms, and I was not in the least bit complaining. Silently I was building the me-and-Sandy story. If I kept my cool, surely I could make it happen. This sort of magical thinking had been a part of me my whole life—I never knew it was unrealistic, in spite of all my plans and designs never turning out just so. I always assumed it hadn't worked because I *hadn't* kept my cool, I had failed somehow to be something or someone this perpetual other was looking for. In reality, even if I could have figured out what trait, what personality characteristic, what *thing* Steven had that I did not (other than obvious biology), it's not as if I could just go pick it up at Wal-Mart. I had so much more to learn.

Things began to unravel very quickly. I drove past Steven's house every day on my way to work. A few times I made the healthy choice of taking a different route. Still, I was fully under the self-delusion that, if I saw her car in his driveway one morning, I'd be perfectly fine with it. Non-monogamy: no harm, no foul.

This sexual equation always made more sense to me if I also had a different lover in these situations, but I rarely did. What really happened was each day I drove past and she *wasn't* there, my confidence she would choose me grew. Then, inevitably, the fragile fantasy I had built so tirelessly cracked wide open. There it was. Her vehicle, *my* lover's car, right there in his driveway for all the world to see. I slowed and checked the license plate, as if I could have been mistaken.

It was way too early in the morning for her to just be dropping by for coffee. I ran through a thousand reasons why she could be there and not have had sex with him, but they were all flimsy and discarded immediately.

Denying my feelings, I bypassed any hurt and went straight to guilt and shame. I had no reason to be jealous over a lover who never promised me anything, and who told me up front she didn't want a commitment. But what about all the terrible things she told me about him? What about every single time she called him an asshole in her discussions with me, her other lover and best friend? I may not have had any rights to feel betrayed, but betrayed I felt. An infantile tantrum and complete emotional breakdown quickly ensued.

I pulled myself together at work. Still unskilled at priorities, though, I was highly distracted, complained to my co-worker friends who would listen, made several phone calls on the company's dime. By the end of the day I'd accomplished zero except to work myself further into a frenzy. I knew I could not talk to her. I could not *not* be cool about this. My freaking out is the very thing she was afraid of, the very reason she had hesitated to "break the make out barrier" that first night. What she wanted was a partner who would roll with the punches, not tie her down, and essentially allow her to do whatever the hell she wanted. I was determined to be that. Anything less would mean losing her, and that was unacceptable to me.

Have you ever tried to be someone or something you inherently are not? If you answered yes, you know it never works. My way to be something I wasn't was to avoid Sandy the whole next day. That gave me enough time, or so I thought, to rebuild my own façade. I was actually surprised to discover there was absolutely no way I was going to avoid this breakup. It was going to happen, with or without me or my consent. Still, I clung to small fragments of hope.

After many tearful conversations, complete with groveling and begging on my part, Sandy decided she needed to be celibate while she "figured things out." That was fine with me, since it meant I was still in the running. I had finally broken down about my discomfort over seeing her at Steven's house, and appealed to her emotionally, told her I'd work on my jealousy and give her space. Aside from not having sex, I continued to treat her as if she were my girlfriend, no different than how I was with her before we had ever tumbled into bed together in the first place. We hung out, watched movies, shared meals, cuddled, etc. Status quo. I completely ignored the fact she was becoming more and more distant—all of our contact was at my initiation. I "acted as if" and waited for the storm to pass.

My next crack in the veneer came when a mutual friend inadvertently and quite innocently told me Sandy had slept with a mutual male friend of ours. Celibacy, my ass. I was so enraged; I laid into my poor friend on the phone and let out a litany of insults I would almost never use, including calling Sandy a whore and wishing she'd rot in hell.

I brought none of my misgivings to *her*, of course. Playing it cool was still my main objective. If only I could be okay with her non-monogamy, I believed we could still work things out, in our friendship, and in a romantic and sexual context. True to my fractured core belief system, I sought tirelessly for what was "wrong with me" and how to fix it. The solution was still the only one I'd come up with many years ago—if I could find a way to magically and willfully change how I *felt* then, somehow, everything would be all right.

The problem with that solution is it never works. I tried my whole life to deny who I was and what I valued only to find it impossible.

Sandy and I grew increasingly uncomfortable around each other. My attempts to exist in the relationship and under these circumstances simply wasn't working. I didn't want to share my lover with anyone else—that was how most of the world felt and I wasn't any different. She, however, had a way of making me feel guilty about this, insinuating if I were more secure with myself, it wouldn't bother me in the slightest.

I believed her. I decided the whole falling apart of us as a "we" instead of a "you and I" was entirely my fault. More guilt, more shame. The harder I tried to convince her I was not a fucking lunatic, the more insane I appeared. Months were spent vacillating between it being all her fault and all mine. Not once did it occur to me it simply didn't work out, that perhaps it just wasn't meant to be. I was a crazed lunatic most of the time. I'd call her or show up at her house, we'd yell at each other, we'd both cry, then we'd both apologize. It was so much *drama*.

But drama was what I lived for, what I thrived on, what proved to me beyond the shadow of a doubt that even if she— or any other *she* for that matter—didn't love me, at least she cared. So desperate for someone to "fix" me, I engaged in this push/pull, run away/come back thing with Sandy for far too long. Even once she moved in with Steven, I still could not, *would* not, let go of the idea that we would be together, we were *meant* to be together. How much more evidence did I need?

Not much. Or *too* much—I suppose that depends on how you look at it. One too many tear-filled confrontations and Sandy finally said to me, "I wish you would just let me go."

I remember standing in her kitchen just being so tired. Sick and tired of being sick and tired, as they say. It takes a lot of energy to hold onto someone who is clearly not yours to hold. You would think I'd have known this by now, but apparently

I'm a slow learner. I don't know what it was about that moment, what made that statement the one to finally sink in, but it did. I was so ashamed of my behavior, so disappointed in myself at how I had treated someone I claimed to love, so much of a thousand other things, I simply surrendered. I walked out of Sandy's house that night and didn't look back for a very, very long time.

We eventually rekindled our friendship years later, but things were never and *can* never be the same. I can tell you today with absolute certainty we were romantically incompatible. Although I believe with all my heart she is a good person, she is not at all what I am looking for in a life partner. Why I couldn't see it then is so complex, so therapy-oriented, so dynamically ingrained within me, it would take a whole other book to explain it.

What matters most is we both moved on. I have forgiven her, and it has ceased to matter whether she has forgiven me. I know today that what really matters is I learned just a little bit more about myself, about love, about relationships. Isn't that always the point?

Chapter 7: Annie
"I'm not that straight."

I THOUGHT I had essentially defeated this pattern in my life. After coming to terms with and spending a few years dealing with my own intimacy issues head-on, I was feeling pretty healthy, rather emotionally fit. I'd given up the pursuit of some fantasy woman I no longer believed existed. Acceptance of myself and my life circumstances exactly as they were was finally within reach. Still single, yes, but dare I say I was actually happy? At the very least, I was content. Things were going well for me; I learned and grew in unimaginable ways. Yes, I believed I was truly on my own road to a destiny unknown, and I was no longer afraid. I was excited.

I met the most amazing woman but didn't yet know she was amazing. I could barely remember her name most of the time. In the beginning, I didn't even find her that attractive. Yet there was something very alluring, all taking place very unconsciously. I had heard her speak at AA meetings a few times, and she seemed very much in tune with my own spiritual belief system. I really believed this was someone who could contribute to and enrich my own journey, so I asked for her phone number.

For weeks, perhaps months, it sat in my wallet without a second thought. Then I heard myself ask a friend, "Is she married?" as my next "unsure," the woman's phone number was in my wallet, walked by me in the parking lot of one of our clubhouses. Deep beneath my layers of denial, the process was already in swing. I didn't acknowledge it for a long time, and even when I did, my claim was to a "harmless crush" when, really, for me, there is no such thing.

I watched a movie with a spiritual theme and suddenly she came to mind, things I had heard her say, beliefs we had discussed. On a total whim, I finally called her. She was out of town on vacation and I offered to let her go, but she insisted. We talked for nearly an hour. Sometimes when I meet people who are my intellectual equivalents, it becomes a mission to place them in my life. If you've ever been highly philosophical, you know how rare it is to find people you can have those kinds of very deep and profound conversations with. These people are rare gems who quickly secure a position of importance in your life—who else are you going to call when you've stumbled upon a great truth that relates to the world at large, to the concepts of faith and humanity?

Still, for a while that magical phone call was a one-time event. We continued to run into each other with alarming frequency but I had not put the pieces together. I called her up to invite her to a social gathering, and didn't hear back from her until a couple of days later. Somehow, though, that return phone call set a precedent, and we began to communicate regularly, both on the phone and sporadically via e-mail.

Every time we talked, I found her to be more and more compelling. She said things like, "I'm not going to have an electronic relationship with you. I'm all about the face-to-face." There was something about the way she communicated that made me feel simultaneously intimate yet distant, in an indescribable way—you would have had to experience it to really understand. She spoke often of a higher concept of love, universal love, God's love, the common thread that runs through all of humanity.

More and more intriguing she became with each interaction, and I grew more and more afraid of where this might be headed. I tried rigorously to live in reality and give myself large doses of the facts: 1) she was married, 2) she had children, 3) she was straight. But no matter how often I acknowledged these things, the greater truth, at least in my life, is love knows no bounds, nor any logic.

Having lived a life of falling in love, I developed the ability to know the exact moment when the shift occurred within me, when desire stood up and demanded to no longer be ignored. With Annie, it happened during a phone call about a book. Different things are bonding for different people. For me, it's literature. If I have loaned you a book, it means I have offered a small piece of myself to you, a window to my soul, for I hold the written word in the highest regard. Unbeknownst to you, I will formulate some deep-seated opinions about you based on your reaction to whatever book of mine you've just read. I loaned Annie my copy of Augusten Burrough's *Magical Thinking,* in my top ten favorites of all time. In discussing the work, she said, "Well, he's funny, but I don't think he's as funny as I think you think he is."

I replied, "Well, I'm also gay, so I can appreciate his humor on that level."

She said, "Oh, I'm not *that* straight." Then, there was a very awkward silence. She followed up with, "Well, I'm not that gay either, but I'm certainly not that straight."

I was dumbfounded. Had she really just said that to me, of all people? Did she have the slightest idea of what she'd just done? I actually posed these questions to her many months later, after conversations much more momentous that this one, and she told me, "I knew exactly who you were and I knew exactly what I was doing."

In my e-mail correspondence with Annie, I threw out a lot of subtle and not-so-subtle romantic undertones. They went unacknowledged, but also not rebuked. Something was happening in this developing friendship deep below the surface, yet neither party was discussing it openly. Then, without any kind of warning, affection was introduced into our relationship.

I had stumbled and fallen outside before a meeting and had this big, purplish bruise on the palm of my hand. When I showed this to her, she took my hand and gently stroked it. In and of itself, this was not a huge deal, but my immediate reaction was to pull away from her, behavior not at all representative of who I usually am with a woman I'm interested in. A little while after that, on the same night, we were seated next to each other around a bonfire with many of our mutual friends, and she teased me about my reaction, joking about my fear of intimacy, which I denied. So she took my hand again, wordlessly, touching my swollen palm with her fingertips but looking at me, saying, "Doesn't that feel good?"

Was she kidding? Was she flirting with me? I couldn't figure her out. Maybe she really was just loving and kind—I didn't know, and I didn't ask. At least, not at that moment, not that night. This was the first time we were in a social setting together for any extended period of time and I wanted to pay close attention to our dynamic and what might really be happening. For days afterward, I asked everyone who knew me and knew how I felt what they had seen, what their perception was because I didn't trust my own. Her attention toward me, her affection with me, all of this was obvious to anyone who was paying attention. But no one could tell me what it meant because she was still straight and still married.

A few days after that bonfire, I broached the topic, scared half to death of what she would say. I questioned her sudden affection, and she told me it was simply her comfort level with me at the time, and the people we were with, that she was just being herself. Okay. So what about my romantic hints, particularly via e-mail…surely they had not gone unnoticed?

She asked me what *I* thought it meant. I said, "Well, either you really are that loving and tolerant of others, or you kind of like it when I do that."

She responded, "What if there's an option C, that the reason I let you do that is a strange combination of both?"

I was emboldened by that, so I pushed forward. "Annie, I think you know how I feel about you. But I wonder if it's at all possible you feel the same way?"

There it was, on the table now, there was no turning back. I waited for her response, knowing all too well by now she had an uncanny talent of being evasive and vague while seeming to answer questions at the same time. What she finally did say was, "Do you have any idea like, the million things that would need to happen to even make that relationship possible?"

Here's what I heard: "It's possible."

The discussion was shelved for the time being. Nothing changed. She had a very full life, so I cherished the moments I was granted when they were available. We'd gotten in the habit of hanging out at a picnic table in a park that, at some point, came to represent my connection with her—we eventually referred to it only as "our" picnic table. She always declined invitations to come to my house, so I stopped asking. I had a roommate at the time, so that didn't bother me; I had more privacy with her at the picnic table. And I could have her all to myself—I think the gay guy who lived with me at the time even had a crush on her, she was just the kind of person everyone fell for, regardless of gender or sexual orientation. So outdoors on a summer night was just fine.

One of those nights she told me her whole story, simply because I'd asked. I was amazed and even a little shocked at some of it, but completely enraptured. I could not imagine her being anyone other than the person I had come to know, but she had been someone else, there was much evidence. I wanted to know everything there was to know about her, not just because I was falling for her, but because no one else seemed to know anything at all.

In our small community that was strange. I had sometimes gotten close to people who were not good for me, who were not healthy and a little bit dangerous for me emotionally, and I'd been hurt in a variety of ways as a result. So I had developed a habit of "running people by" others I was close to and trusted. I had done this with Annie, and I couldn't find one person who knew anything about her. This should have been a warning siren, but instead I just thought it made her mysterious which, to me, was incredibly sexy.

Sharing your life story with someone else is an intimate affair, so it made me feel special she would share hers with me. I made mental notes about a handful of things: although she didn't come right out and say it, she gave enough clues to a well-trained ear to let me know she was a trauma survivor. I guessed sexual assault at some point in her youth. She also made it very clear she was unhappy in her marriage and had been for some time—she had essentially married her drug dealer, not uncommon for an addicted woman, and it was a total fluke they both happened to get sober together.

That was seventeen years ago, and clearly they had grown apart in immeasurable ways. I got the distinct feeling she was a completely different person than she had been, and not just in the generic way that all recovering people are. There was something more, something deep and unseen I felt privileged to glimpse. She was an addict of a rare breed in that she sailed her way through higher education and a steady career track throughout her addiction—she achieved, and achieved big.

While we were having that conversation, I was acutely aware of thoughts running around in my head like, "God, she's beautiful," and "How could anyone lose interest or stop loving her?" and, of course, "I think I could love her and she could love me." I said none of these things out loud but knew from experience it was likely written all over my face. That night, seeing her vulnerability for the first time may have been our truest moment in all those months to come.

On the morning of my fifth anniversary of sobriety, she showed up at my house on her way to work just to hug me. She'd never been inside; she'd been outside once or twice picking up my roommate, who she'd hired to do some cleaning. Extra cash for him, and I got to hear all the details of the inside of her house, like a common voyeur. Somehow we wound up spending more and more time together—locations changed from the picnic table to random rendezvous at restaurants, bookstores, coffee shops. Still never my home or hers, but I knew it would follow eventually as a matter of course.

We developed the kind of friendship where, if I arrived somewhere among mutual friends without her, or she without me, someone would inquire about the other one's whereabouts. And we always knew the answer. "She's taking her son to so-and-so," or "she's working late," or "I just talked to her, she'll be here soon."

We had the information on each other because we were in practically constant contact. Over the course of a day, it was rare for me to not speak with her at least twice, usually more, via e-mail, text messaging, or old fashioned phone calls, which were my favorite because I longed to hear her voice on a continuous basis.

I convinced myself and others what I was doing was perfectly fine, totally harmless. I justified that my lesson was to love unconditionally, without expectations, love for love's sake, enjoying for a while the light-heartedness that comes with being crazy in love and getting to see and be with the object of your adoration all the time. Not once did she seem uncomfortable with the idea I was in love with her—we spoke of it openly, and she denied me nothing of my own feelings and desires. I was free to love her if that was what I wanted to do.

This was a brand new experience for me. Unrequited love was not at all new, but the occurrence of unrequited love absent of a constant feeling of rejection was entirely foreign. How wonderful to have ridiculously fallen for someone, and then have the pleasure of telling that very person all about it and they never even bat an eye. She never rebuked a hug, never once said, "Please don't say so-and-so to me," and rarely commented when I was engaged in my most vulnerable professions or confessions. She would gently set boundaries when I verbally crossed certain lines of flirtation but, overall, I felt very safe, and that was new.

The longer I stayed on, and the further I risked in telling her my feelings, the more secure I became she would not turn heel and run. For someone with my particular brand of abandonment issues, this was a pure joy.

But that joy did not last. The longer our relationship continued, the more obsessed I became. Every waking moment was dedicated to figuring out if and how I could get her to be with me. She began to throw out subtle reminders of her inherent heterosexuality—remarking about attractive men, making reference to her love of hetero sex. Every time she did, I ignored it in favor of some other mixed message she had either given me verbally or physically. Once she was at my house—we did, of course, graduate to that—and when I hugged her, she pulled away from me. "That's new, that thing you're doing. Please don't do that."

I hung my head in shame and apologized profusely. I wasn't entirely aware of what I was apologizing for, but I had a pretty good idea. My embraces with her had become more sensual; it had happened as a matter of progression on an entirely unconscious level. When I put my arms around her, I put one hand on the small of her back. This little thing makes a huge difference for two intensely emotional people.

I decided to play this a different way; in other words, I made a conscious decision to try and manipulate her. Shortly after she left, I called and said, "I felt so bad but now I'm not exactly sure what I'm apologizing for."

She said, "If you really don't know, then I'll show you the next time I see you."

And she did. The next time I saw her; she hugged me and placed my hands on the small of her back with her own. She took control of the very thing she had asked me not to do. I would have congratulated myself on tricking her into letting me do that except I knew she was too smart to be tricked. This was the exact level of subtlety that lurked beneath every interaction between us—every word, every hug, every look that ever passed between us was heavily loaded in a very exciting, but very dangerous, way.

The next time we were at my house, alone, she verbally announced what I took to be an acknowledgement of possibility. We were sitting far too close to each other on my couch and talking about her uncanny ability to be right about things 98% of the time, at least when it came to her judgments about *other* people and what she thought they would do or say. "For example," she said, "I know things about you that you don't even know."

"Oh?" I replied.

"Yeah. Like, if you keep hugging me like that, eventually you're going to kiss me. Hugging like that can only go in one direction."

I almost spit out my sip of Diet Coke. Because she didn't say, "You're going to *try* and kiss me." She had said, "You're *going* to kiss me."

By now I automatically took apart every sentence she uttered to look for clues. This was a huge one. Every time she opened her mouth to speak, I had to go through a whole translation process in my head. It was thoroughly exhausting yet so damn exciting, I had no intention of stopping.

Unusual as her comment was, I was speechless and just let it sort of hang in the air between us. After a few minutes, she asked, "Are you okay?"

Carefully I said, "Yeah. I'm just sitting here trying to figure out why I thought it was okay for me to start hugging you like that in the first place."

She responded, "Well, if you don't know, I'm not going to tell you."

I took that to mean, "Obviously I've given you physical cues to let you know when it's okay to move closer." If I were writing my story with Annie as a screenplay, there would have to be an omniscient offstage voice as a narrator.

This hugging incident was not the first, nor would it be the last, time we had some sort of interaction that was seemingly innocent on the surface but shrouded in innuendos just beneath. Once toward the beginning of our friendship, she and I were waiting at our friend's house for a group of other people to show up for another bonfire. It didn't make sense we'd gotten there before our friend, and as I stood there perplexed at how that had happened, she looked into my eyes, standing less than a foot away from me, and said, "Maybe we're supposed to be here alone."

We stood there, eyes locked, and it was the first time I'd had the conscious and very real impulse to kiss her. I didn't, for no other reason than I was afraid. It was chilly outside, so I asked her if she wanted to wait in the car. "No." I asked if she wanted my jacket. "No." I asked if she wanted a hug. "Yes."

She leaned into my embrace and neither of us said anything. Then there were headlights in the driveway and that moment was over. It felt like we were teenagers who just got caught making out under the bleachers at the football field.

The next day, I confessed to her on the phone and described what that moment had been like for me. "I really wanted to kiss you."

She said, "I know. I was there."

Did that mean, "I sensed you were standing there wanting to kiss me," or did it mean "I know because I also wanted to kiss you?" Everything was always a question with Annie and, internally, my questions always led to more questions and never any answers.

Then she added, "But that wouldn't work because if you tried to kiss me, I would have had to reject you and it would have sucked for both of us."

Again, I analyze. Would it suck for her because she had to reject me but didn't want to? I never asked those questions out loud, and even if I had, I wouldn't have gotten a straight answer. Or rather, I would have gotten a "straight" answer.

Some time after the great hug debate, we were alone together at a neutral location near an AA clubhouse after a meeting. While we were talking, and earlier during the meeting, I'd noticed her making gestures that suggested some sort of cramp in her shoulder or neck. Another opportunity. I said, "You know I'd be happy to give you a back rub."

Of course that's what I said—who in their right mind would say anything but that to a woman who they were addicted to touching and fantasizing about? We spent the next twenty minutes discussing all the reasons why me giving her a back rub was a bad idea. Then we had a conversation about my current feelings for her, ideas I'd had in my head for a week. I worked up the nerve to say to her, "So, here's what I think. I believe you can wrap you're head around the idea of having sex with me, but you can't handle the idea of having an actual committed relationship with me."

These conversations always revolved around some magical future, where she was divorced from her husband and neither of us was being dishonest about what was or wasn't happening between us. Her response to that was, "I'm not going to sleep with you. And the reason I won't is because I'm pretty committed to not hurting you."

To me this meant the reason she wouldn't wasn't because she didn't want to. While I was reveling in my interpretation, she said, "Okay, I'm ready for that massage now." She winked and came over to sit in front of me. Unbelievable.

Touching Annie in any sort of way that even remotely resembled intimacy, or sexuality, or both, was downright electric for me. However, those electrical charges were usually short, due to the nature of our supposed platonic relationship. Every once in a while she'd hold my hand while we were sitting together, or let me put my arm around her, both of which, in her mind, were things which she would do with other heterosexual female friends as signs of kinship and affection. She was, after all, a physically affectionate person. A handful of times she'd even played with my hair, very much a "girlfriends" thing.

The problem was that I was *not* one of her heterosexual friends, a fine point we both continued to ignore or, at the very least, overlook, in order to serve our own needs. It was quite interesting to me that, primarily, she was prone to touching me more when we were in a social setting with others, which made me incredibly uncomfortable. I think she believed if she touched me in front of other people, it was proof it was innocent and platonic affection.

I, on the other hand, initiated touching much more often when we were alone, because we both knew what I wanted from her and I wasn't ashamed of it if no one else was there to see it.

That night when I was rubbing her neck and shoulders, the tension was palpable. To this day, I don't know if that's how it was for her. I don't truly know how any of it was for her, in retrospect. For me, massaging is a skill I've developed through many relationships that involved physical contact, both romantic and platonic. In other words, I knew what I was doing, and I knew I was good at it.

I don't know how many minutes passed without either of us saying anything. It was so clear to me where I wanted this to go, what I wanted to happen next. But nothing had changed. She was still married (although leaning a little more toward divorce every day), she was still straight, and I had absolutely no business doing what I was doing, let alone taking it further.

Still, that close contact overrode any rational thought I might have had. All I could think about was how I was going to do what I was about to do. I gently brushed her hair back from the nape of her neck.

Just as I was about to kiss her exposed throat, my fucking cell phone rang!

It was after midnight on a Friday and anyone who knew me at all would know I was in the presence of my adored one and should *not* be disturbed. For a split second I thought about not answering it. Then I thought, if someone is calling me this late, it must be important. It fucking *better* be important. "Hello?" I said, but I didn't move an inch from my location, still right up against her backside with my hand on her shoulder.

It *was* important. My friend's boyfriend was having some trouble breathing, and "just didn't feel right" and he had suffered a heart attack just a few weeks prior. They were sure it was probably nothing, but called to see if I'd drive him to the ER. He was scared.

Still selfish to the core, I tried to beg off, "Does he *really* need to go? What do you think? Can it wait?"

Now I had one hand on Annie's shoulder and my forehead pressed to her back, knowing I had to go, knowing there was not a good enough reason I could come up with to not drive someone to the ER. I never should have answered the phone. To this day, I still wonder what would have happened that night. I was never to have quite that exact same opportunity again.

And my relationship with Annie was already closer to the end than I knew. Friends without cars with boyfriends with bad hearts. Divine intervention does indeed happen in mysterious ways.

It was during the holiday season, right in the middle of peace on earth and good will toward men, that the D word (divorce) finally found its way into Annie's own living room. On Christmas Eve, she called me while I was gift giving and celebrating joy at my friend Jessy's house. I could tell the moment I heard her voice that something was wrong. "Are you going to the 8 o'clock meeting?" she asked.

Jessy was looking at me with that, "It's *her*, isn't it?" look. I stepped into the bathroom with my cell phone. "Annie, what's up? I wasn't planning on going to the meeting, why?"

She slowly explained to me she was going down to the hall with her husband. I was baffled. "Why are you calling and telling me this?"

Apparently, I was supposed to know already. "Did it ever occur to you the reason I'm calling is because I need people to be there who are in my corner?"

Oh. This was a call for support—how foolish of me to have assumed otherwise. "I'll see you there," I said and hung up the phone. I went back into the living room and looked guiltily at Jessy.

I didn't have to say who it was or where I was going. "Just be careful," she said, and hugged me goodbye.

That meeting I went and met Annie at was from that moment forward referred to as the "Divorce Meeting." I got to the hall five minutes before the meeting started and didn't have time to talk to her. I sat at the table in front of her, directly across the room from her husband. Once all the drunks with their coffee cups were settled into their seats, we did our customary readings, and the table was open for any problem, topic, or solution related to alcoholism.

Sometimes at these meetings, whoever "shares" first sets a precedent for a topic. The very first person to share at this particular meeting began the discussion by talking about how hard it was to be going through a divorce at this time of year. One by one, the next three people who spoke all talked about divorces past and present, and how it affected their alcoholic lives. Slowly and as discretely as possible, I turned around in my chair to find Annie staring directly at me, with a look that clearly said, "Can you fucking believe this?!"

I looked back across the room at her husband, completely oblivious to the irony. I sat through the next forty-five minutes aware of nothing else than the feeling of her, knowing she was looking at me, right behind me.

After the meeting, everyone socialized and worked on puzzles and played cards, a festive bunch gathered in camaraderie. Annie and I sat next to each other with a group of four or five others and worked on building gingerbread houses. I swore sometimes AA felt like "arts and crafts" for adults. We spoke about the divorce meeting only in coded language and facial expressions, but I knew exactly what she was thinking. The time had come. She had waited for years for God to show her a sign, and this was it.

When I watched her leave with him that night, I knew I would get a phone call a few hours later detailing everything that transpired from the moment they walked out the door. "So here's how it happened," Annie was saying as I dragged myself out of bed for a glass of water and a cigarette. She relayed the entire conversation she'd had with her husband on the way home.

As if the meeting itself had not been enough, right before they left, a friend of her husband's had said, "You know, not that long ago, I heard a rumor you two were getting divorced." When they got in their car to drive home, he started to comment about it, and she interrupted him by blurting out that, although it was just a rumor, for her there was some truth in it. And the emotional journey of taking apart a marriage had begun.

I had no delusions Annie's desire for divorce had anything in the least to do with me. However, what I imagined could happen afterward had everything to do with me. Somewhere deep inside all along I knew the truth—what I wanted more than anything would never, could never, be. But I refused to swallow that truth for the next several months as I watched her dismantle her entire normal, married complete-with-kids, country club styled, well-financed life.

I tried very hard to set my feelings for her aside and be a good friend through a difficult time. Some days I managed that better than others. But the feeling of her drifting away from me little by little was happening, and there was no amount of denial that could shield me from seeing it, from knowing it. True to my lifelong patterns, the only thing I knew how to do was try harder, redouble my efforts, cling tighter—all behaviors that were in direct conflict with what she wanted or needed from any friend *or* lover. I could not stand aside from myself long enough to see that; it was impossible to even try and separate emotion from action. I was in love with her, and would be for a very long time, even after she was gone.

I hung on. I listened to every heart wrenching phone call in silence, not knowing how to help, not knowing how to comfort. She was sad and depressed, so one evening I invited her to my house to watch a DVD season of *Sex and the City*, something I knew would cheer her up. We'd originally made plans to go see a movie, but she just wasn't up for that. Fine by me—I always did whatever she wanted anyhow, like a puppy. A happy, grateful, head-over-heels puppy. She wanted the last episode of the sixth season, the plot being the relationship between the lead character and the Russian artist. At one point in that episode, Carrie makes a passionate speech about what it is she's looking for in love, so similar to conversations Annie and I had had, I wondered if I'd actually written this script in some sort of magic-induced blackout and had forgotten.

Annie was sprawled out on my love seat, and I was in my easy chair. I silently wept with complete recognition. She had no plan whatsoever of pursuing what was being described on my TV screen with me. I knew there were other men, or at least one other man that she was interested in—I'd known that all along. So here we were, together in silence while Sarah Jessica Parker voiced an impassioned rendition of what fantasies love holds for everyone. Of what she as a person, not a character, quite likely wanted, what I wanted, what Annie wanted, what every human being longs for most of their lives. Some are lucky enough to find it, but I surely wasn't, and neither was Annie. I had believed I could find it in her; I don't know if she believed she could or ever would find it in anyone.

There were no words for me to say as the credits rolled on

the DVD and I wiped away my tears, hoping she could not see but at the same time guiltily wishing she could. Dignity versus desire, always my ultimate battle.

When I got up to turn off the TV and eject the DVD, my mind was no longer in control of my next several actions. I went to her, sat down next to her on the love seat, and took her hand. There wasn't anything I wanted more in that moment than to put my head upon her chest and have her arms around me, protected from the world and everything in it. In the middle of the chaos of her life and everything she had been through in recent months—a pending divorce, childhoods of her two boys disrupted in shattering ways, immense fear at undoing everything it took her eighteen years to build—through all of it, in that moment I could still only think of what I wanted from her. That, as they say, is the straw that broke the camel's back.

She recoiled from me immediately and got up to leave. It was a horrible moment I would always wish I could take back. Standing at the door, I said, "Wait, please wait. I don't understand. You allow me to do things like that all the time, but then act as if you don't want me to, or it makes you uncomfortable. For God's sake, just say, 'it makes me uncomfortable,' if it does."

And she did. Not only did she tell me I'd made her uncomfortable, she told me the way I behaved was exactly the opposite of what she needed from me, which was for me to be respectful and physically distant, to truly be a friend and just be with her through the grief of her process, to be supportive without exploiting how I might benefit from her sorrow. She walked out of my home that night for the last time.

I was frightened she really would leave and never come back, so I didn't attempt to contact her for the next two days. When I did, it was in the form of an e-mail, which I knew she hated, almost as if I was ensuring the outcome I claimed to have feared the most. I typed only, "Are you gone?"

She replied, "I'm not sure yet."

That night she called me and said, "I can't do this. This

whole love/friendship thing, it's too hard, I just can't."

Of course I begged, pleaded, cried, bargained; I ran through the whole five stages of grief in less than five minutes. She wasn't having any of it—she kept things brief and said she had intentionally called me because she knew I had somewhere to be that night. A friend was outside blowing the horn for me while over the phone, she was ending a relationship I had invested my very soul in. How is it possible the most horrific breakup I've ever been through was with a woman I was never really with?

Devastated, I carried out my social plans for the evening, whining and crying to anyone who would listen to me. I called Annie immediately when I got home, and she refused to answer the phone. I left three messages at fifteen minute intervals, then cried myself to sleep. The next several months were very much the same. I would quit her like a drug, only to "relapse" and try and make contact, then feel ten times worse afterward. I ignored any request she might have made for me to stop contacting her, then felt consummately guilty about that, too. Like both real and fantasy relationships that preceded her, I went back and forth—it's her fault, it's my fault, she's a bitch, I'm a fool, she took advantage of me, I wasn't respectful of what she was going through, etc., ad infinitum.

Since we had mutual friends I would run into her without warning. The first time, she did give me some notice. She actually called and told me she'd be at the next bonfire. I kept her on the phone as long as I could, but she only said, "Let's just trust the universe."

I didn't—I could not bring myself to trust in something that had taken the woman I loved away from me, whether that was God, the universe, karma, whatever; it made no difference. When I saw her that night, I didn't even acknowledge her the first few times we crossed paths, then, in desperation, when she walked past me in the kitchen, I said her name. She stopped and turned. I asked, "Can I have a hug?"

"Yes."

I went to her and put my arms around her for a few moments, then we were interrupted by someone coming through the back door of the house. The rest of the night went by without further interaction and, like a crack addict fresh out of a twenty-eight day rehab, when I returned home that night I called her repeatedly, leaving begging, pleading, humiliating messages.

It was devastating to watch myself behave this way, but I just couldn't stop. Every chance I got, I took. I'd see her at a meeting, then send a text message, saying things like, "I saw you were wearing the bracelet I gave you. That meant a lot to me." Or the occasional e-mail stating, "I know you don't want to talk to me and that's fine, but I want you to know I still care about you, and I hope you are doing well."

Annie's determination to strip me from her life in any form or fashion may have been her greatest asset. She knew, and I knew (even though I denied it), that if she gave me even a centimeter, I would have taken a mile. All things considered, I should have sent her a thank you card for walking out of my life. But you know what they say about hindsight.

I can't tell you exactly how long it went on, or how I finally arrived at a place of letting go, only that I did eventually, and not without extreme amounts of pain and despair ultimately leading to what is always at the end of the road: surrender. I have enough distance to be almost ambivalent about it. I have no knowledge of how she feels about me now, or how she really felt about me then, and it has ceased to matter.

For most of my life I believed I had to *understand* something in order to let it go. That simply isn't true—life just happens, and sometimes we get what we want, or what we think we want, and sometimes we don't. Ironically, the most significant thing I can say about my relationship with Annie is it taught me enough lessons, it brought me enough cleansing pain, that I became willing to face demons, to acknowledge my part in the pattern that haunted me for years. More importantly, as a result of that process, I was able to write this book, and share it with you. For that, I am truly grateful.

Afterword

IN TWELVE-STEP PROGRAMS all over the world for every obsessive and compulsive habit known to mankind, there is a common sentiment:

"No matter how far down the scale we have gone, we will see how our experience can benefit others." (Alcoholics Anonymous, p.84)

I have known this to be true in many areas of my life, both in what I have been able to share with others and with what they have shared with me. Assuming I am not the only lesbian on earth who has fallen in love repeatedly with unavailable women, "mostly" heterosexual or not, I can only hope the belief holds true—that if I can share it with you and you are like me, perhaps you'll feel just a little less alone in the world. Perhaps it will give you some hope to know that, in all these years, I have not given up the fight for romantic love.

Although my romantic history is checkered with an equal number of relationships with women who identify as lesbian, I chose to bring *this* group of stories to print. Perhaps I think they are more interesting, or have more humor. However, it is more likely there's a healing within myself that needed to occur. Therapeutic processes are widely varied, but I suspect most other writers would tell you that, in recording any sort of personal memoir, there is a time of emotional introspection. Writing about these women I've known has given me great pause and a chance to revisit and do battle with some of my own demons along the way. Relationships are part of the sustenance of our very lives, our very existence.

Between the lines of the stories there is a narrative of personal growth, a coming to terms with my own character flaws, and facing the truth beneath why I "chose" these women in the first place. Having endured enough therapy around my "issues" makes it impossible to see myself as a victim in these relationships. Although I've been hurt and even occasionally given hurt in return, it is I who remains the common denominator. At some point I had to become willing to ask, "Why?" The answers to that are the answers that belong to me; yours might very well be different. The stories in this book are not about blame or fault; after all, it takes two people to create, maintain, or ultimately destroy a relationship, no matter how intimate or casual.

I hope this book brought you to a better understanding, and maybe even acceptance and a little bit of forgiveness in your own story, with your own characters, told within your own heart of experience.

Angela Kelly

About the Author

ANGELA KELLY HAS been writing since she was tall enough to hit the keys on a manual typewriter. Two of her poems, "Religion" and "Redemption," have been published, and other works have appeared in a variety of independent magazines and newsletters. *Unavailable* is her first novel-length book.

Kelly lives, breathes, and consumes books. She has been employed in the publishing production industry for over ten years, and has a Bachelor's degree in English from the University of Illinois. She spends much of her time haunting libraries and local bookstores, always in search of the next piece of inspiring and overwhelming literature to add to her reading repertoire.

A native Jersey girl, Kelly currently resides begrudgingly in the cornfields of the Midwest with her partner, Cindy, and their furry four-legged children. She hopes to someday retire near the ocean of the east coast, where she plans to write her memoirs with a sharp shell in the sand.

For more information about Angela Kelly, visit her website at angelakelly.wordpress.com.